creating résumés, letters, business cards, and flyers in Word

Visual QuickProject Guide

by Maria Langer

Peachpit
Press

Visual QuickProject Guide

Creating Résumés, Letters, Business Cards, and Flyers in Word
Maria Langer

Peachpit Press

1249 Eighth Street
Berkeley, CA 94710
510/524-2178
800/283-9444
510/524-2221 (fax)

Find us on the World Wide Web at: www.peachpit.com
To report errors, please send a note to errata@peachpit.com
Peachpit Press is a division of Pearson Education

Editor: Nancy Davis
Production Editor: Lisa Brazieal
Compositor: Maria Langer
Indexer: Julie Bess
Cover design: The Visual Group with Aren Howell
Interior design: Elizabeth Castro
Cover photo credit: Photodisc

Notice of Rights

Notice of Liability

Trademarks

ISBN 0-321-24751-5

9 8 7 6 5 4 3 2 1

Printed and bound in the United States of America

To Mike,
on the 20th anniversary
of our engagement.

I still love you.

Special Thanks to...

Nancy Davis, for thinking of me for this great project—my first color book! And for helping me keep on track throughout the writing and production process.

Lisa Brazieal, for helping me fine-tune the book's layout and appearance.

Julie Bess, for coming to my rescue when I needed an index on short notice (again).

Microsoft Corporation, for continuing to improve the world's best word processing program for Windows and Macintosh users.

To Mike, for the usual things.

contents

contents

contents

introduction

This Visual QuickProject Guide offers a unique way to learn about new technologies. Instead of drowning you in theoretical possibilities and lengthy explanations, this Visual QuickProject Guide uses big, color illustrations coupled with clear, concise step-by-step instructions to show you how to complete a few specific projects in a matter of hours.

Our projects in this book are to create Word documents that you can use to simplify and improve your working life. Why go to a print shop to create letterhead and business cards? Or a graphic designer to create flyers? Why address envelopes by hand? If you have Microsoft Word, you can do it all yourself and make it look great. After all, Word is more than just a glorified typewriter. It has all the tools you need to create useful, professional-looking documents that bring out the best of you and your business.

Word may be the most useful program you have in your computer. It empowers you to tap into your own creativity. In doing so, not only will you save money, but you'll retain complete control over the documents you create. For example, suppose you follow the instructions in Chapter 3 to create a personal or business letterhead template. Three months later, the phone company changes your area code. Or your ISP goes out of business and you get a new e-mail address. Making changes to your letterhead template is as simple as editing a Word file. There's no need to pay a print shop to correct and reprint hundreds of sheets of letterhead paper that you'll have to throw away. And no need to compromise your professionalism by making hand-written corrections to your letterhead while waiting for new letterhead to arrive.

That's one example of how using Word to create these documents can help you. As you work through the projects in this book, you'll learn even more.

what you'll create

Create a custom letterhead template with formatted text.

Import and resize an image or logo to reinforce your company identity.

Prepare a professionally formatted résumé that'll help you get an interview for your next job.

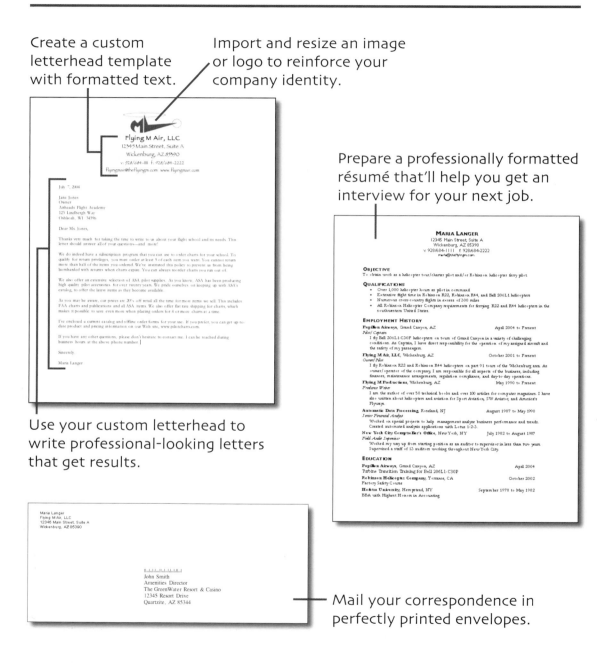

Use your custom letterhead to write professional-looking letters that get results.

Mail your correspondence in perfectly printed envelopes.

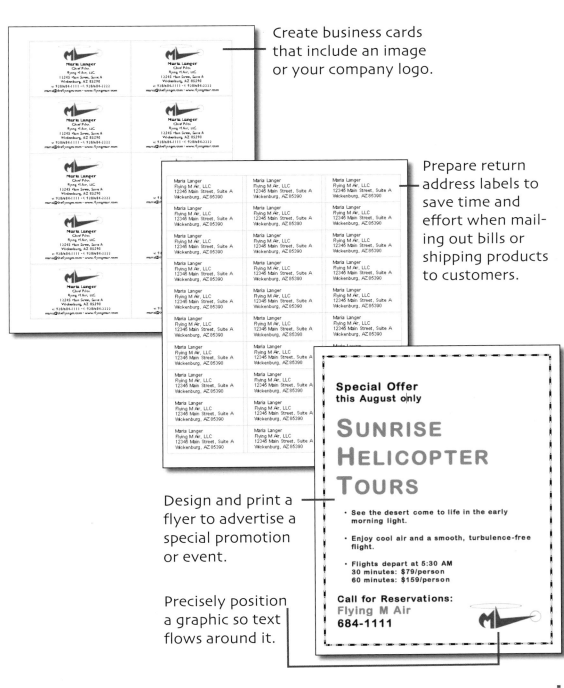

Create business cards that include an image or your company logo.

Prepare return address labels to save time and effort when mailing out bills or shipping products to customers.

Design and print a flyer to advertise a special promotion or event.

Precisely position a graphic so text flows around it.

how this book works

The title of each section explains what is covered on that page.

An introductory sentence or paragraph summarizes what you'll do.

align text

The letterhead text will look better if centered at the top of the page.

Numbered steps explain actions to perform in a specific order.

1 Drag the mouse pointer over the letterhead text to select it.

Important terms, names of interface elements, and text you should type exactly as shown appear in orange.

2 In Windows, click the Center button on the Formatting toolbar...

...or in Mac OS, click the Align Center button in the Alignment and Spacing area of the Formatting palette.

You may have to click this triangle to display Alignment and Spacing options.

Captions explain what you're seeing and why. They also point to relevant parts of Word's interface.

The selected text is centered between the margins.

create a letterhead template 45

The extra bits section at the end of each chapter contains additional tips and tricks that you might like to know—but that aren't absolutely necessary.

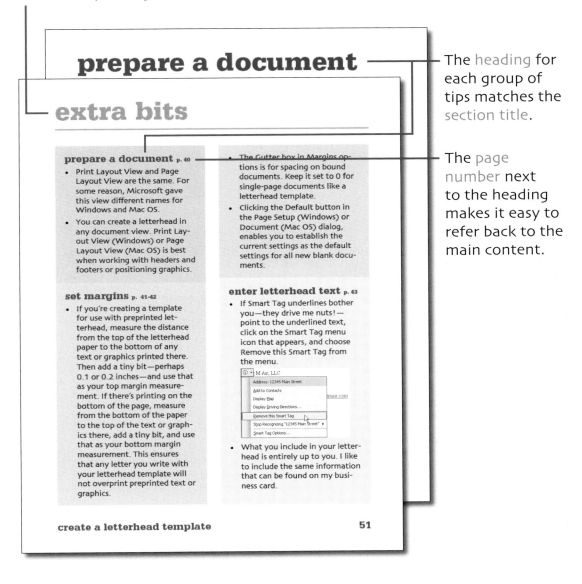

The heading for each group of tips matches the section title.

The page number next to the heading makes it easy to refer back to the main content.

prepare a document

extra bits

prepare a document p. 40
- Print Layout View and Page Layout View are the same. For some reason, Microsoft gave this view different names for Windows and Mac OS.
- You can create a letterhead in any document view. Print Layout View (Windows) or Page Layout View (Mac OS) is best when working with headers and footers or positioning graphics.

set margins p. 41-42
- If you're creating a template for use with preprinted letterhead, measure the distance from the top of the letterhead paper to the bottom of any text or graphics printed there. Then add a tiny bit—perhaps 0.1 or 0.2 inches—and use that as your top margin measurement. If there's printing on the bottom of the page, measure from the bottom of the paper to the top of the text or graphics there, add a tiny bit, and use that as your bottom margin measurement. This ensures that any letter you write with your letterhead template will not overprint preprinted text or graphics.

- The Gutter box in Margins options is for spacing on bound documents. Keep it set to 0 for single-page documents like a letterhead template.
- Clicking the Default button in the Page Setup (Windows) or Document (Mac OS) dialog, enables you to establish the current settings as the default settings for all new blank documents.

enter letterhead text p. 43
- If Smart Tag underlines bother you—they drive me nuts!— point to the underlined text, click on the Smart Tag menu icon that appears, and choose Remove this Smart Tag from the menu.

M Air, LLC
Address: 12345 Main Street
Add to Contacts
Display Map
Display Driving Directions...
Remove this Smart Tag
Stop Recognizing "12345 Main Street"
Smart Tag Options...

- What you include in your letterhead is entirely up to you. I like to include the same information that can be found on my business card.

create a letterhead template   51

the web site

Find this book's companion Web site at:
http://www.langerbooks.com/wordquickproject/.

Content is up-
dated regularly
with news, tips,
and more.

Read timely
articles about
getting the most
out of Word.

Download
sample files
used in the
book.

Access other
valuable online
resources.

Share your com-
ments and tips
with other site
visitors.

the next step

While this Visual QuickProject Guide will walk you through all of the steps required to create letterhead, letters, business cards, résumés, flyers, envelopes, and labels, there's more to learn about Word. After you complete your documents, consider picking up one of my books about Word—Microsoft Office Word 2003 for Windows: Visual QuickStart Guide or Microsoft Word 2004 for Macintosh: Visual QuickStart Guide—as a handy, in-depth reference.

MARIA LANGER

VISUAL QUICKSTART GUIDE

MICROSOFT OFFICE

WORD

FOR WINDOWS

2003

Teach yourself Word the quick and easy way! This Visual QuickStart Guide uses ...tures rather than lengthy ...lanations. You'll be up ...d running in no time!

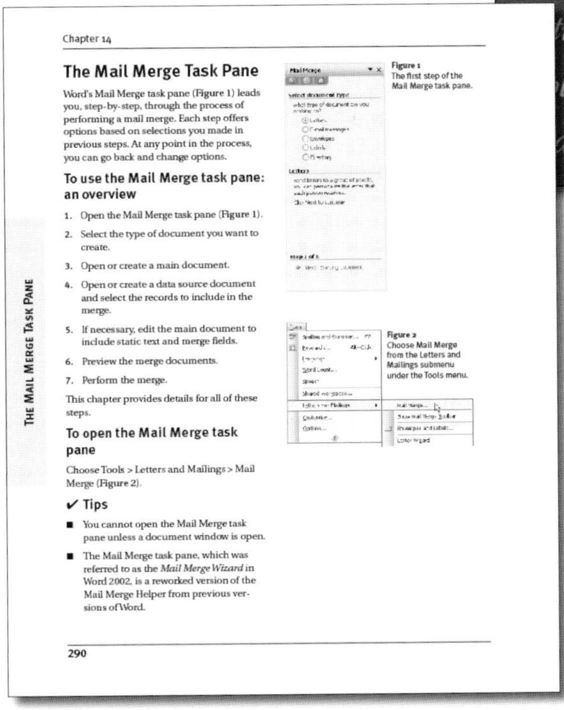

Both books include more advanced information about using Word to create documents. They tell you about all the options you see in Word dialogs, explain how to customize Word so it works the way you need it to, and provide detailed, step-by-step instructions for using basic, intermediate, and advanced Word features.

Chapter 14

The Mail Merge Task Pane

Word's Mail Merge task pane (Figure 1) leads you, step-by-step, through the process of performing a mail merge. Each step offers options based on selections you made in previous steps. At any point in the process, you can go back and change options.

To use the Mail Merge task pane: an overview

1. Open the Mail Merge task pane (Figure 1).
2. Select the type of document you want to create.
3. Open or create a main document.
4. Open or create a data source document and select the records to include in the merge.
5. If necessary, edit the main document to include static text and merge fields.
6. Preview the merge documents.
7. Perform the merge.

This chapter provides details for all of these steps.

To open the Mail Merge task pane

Choose Tools > Letters and Mailings > Mail Merge (Figure 2).

✔ Tips

■ You cannot open the Mail Merge task pane unless a document window is open.

■ The Mail Merge task pane, which was referred to as the *Mail Merge Wizard* in Word 2002, is a reworked version of the Mail Merge Helper from previous versions of Word.

Figure 1
The first step of the Mail Merge task pane.

Figure 2
Choose Mail Merge from the Letters and Mailings submenu under the Tools menu.

290

1. meet microsoft word

Microsoft Word is a full-featured word processing program that you can use to create all kinds of text-based documents, including the letters, résumés, business cards, flyers, and labels you'll create with this book.

As you work with Word, you'll see that it has a lot of the same interface elements you're familiar with from using your other Windows or Mac OS programs: windows, menus, dialogs, and buttons. And, as you work your way through this book you'll see that the Windows and Mac OS versions of Word are remarkably similar—so similar that instructions for one version of the program usually work for the other.

In this chapter, I introduce you to Word's interface elements and tell you about the techniques you'll need to know to use Word. If this project is your first hands-on experience with Word or your computer, be sure to read through this chapter!

This book covers Word 2003 for Windows…

…and Word 2004 for Macintosh.

But if you have an earlier version of Word, you should still be able to follow most of the instructions in this book.

learn the lingo

Before you start working with Word, let me review a few of the terms I'll use throughout this book. If you've been working with your computer for a while, this may seem a bit basic, but I do want to make sure we're on the same page (so to speak) as we work through this project.

An icon is a graphical representation of a file.

WINWORD   Microsoft Word

Here's what the Word program icons look like in Windows (left) and Mac OS X (right).

Letter   Letter

And here's what a Word document icon looks like in Windows (left) and Mac OS X (right).

Windows Explorer is the Windows program that you use to work with files.

If you need to learn more about using Windows, be sure to check out Windows XP: Visual QuickStart Guide by Chris Fehily.

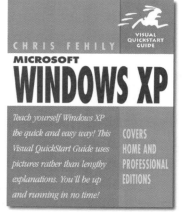

Finder is the Mac OS program that you use to work with files.

If you need to learn how to use Mac OS X, check out Mac OS X Panther: Visual Quick-Start Guide by Maria Langer. (Yes, that's me.)

meet microsoft word

mouse around

The white (Windows) or black (Mac OS) arrow that appears on your screen is the mouse pointer. Move your mouse and the mouse pointer moves.

Point means to position the tip of the mouse pointer on something. For example, you can point to a menu,...

...point to a button,...

...or point to some selected text.

The mouse pointer can also change its appearance when you point to other things. For example, if you point to text or a text area of a Word document window, it changes into an I-beam pointer. ————————— Fourscore and seven years

You use the button(s) on your computer's mouse to click, double-click, and drag.

Click means to press and release the left mouse button on a Windows computer or the only mouse button on a Mac OS computer.

Right-click means to press and release the right mouse button on a Windows computer. (You can't right-click on a Mac unless your Mac has a two-button mouse.)

Double-click means to click twice fast— without moving the mouse between clicks.

Drag means to point to something, hold the mouse button down, and move the mouse. You use this technique to move icons, select text, and perform other tasks.

A typical Windows mouse has two buttons.

A standard Mac OS mouse has only one button. On the Apple Pro Mouse shown here, the whole top of the mouse is a button.

start or open word

In Windows, you start a program. In Mac OS, you open a program. To keep things simple, I'll use the word start for both platforms.

In Windows:

1 Click Start to display the Start menu.

2 Click All Programs.

3 Click Microsoft Office.

4 Click Microsoft Office Word 2003.

Word starts and an untitled document window appears, as shown on page 5.

In Mac OS:

1 Double-click your hard disk icon to open its window.

2 Double-click Applications.

3 Double-click Microsoft Office 2004.

4 Double-click Microsoft Word.

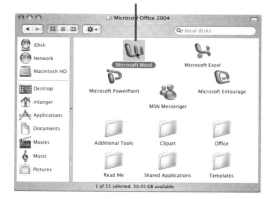

Word starts. If a Project Gallery window appears, click Cancel to dismiss it. An untitled document window appears, as shown on page 6.

meet microsoft word

look at word (Windows)

Here are some of the important interface elements in Word for Windows.

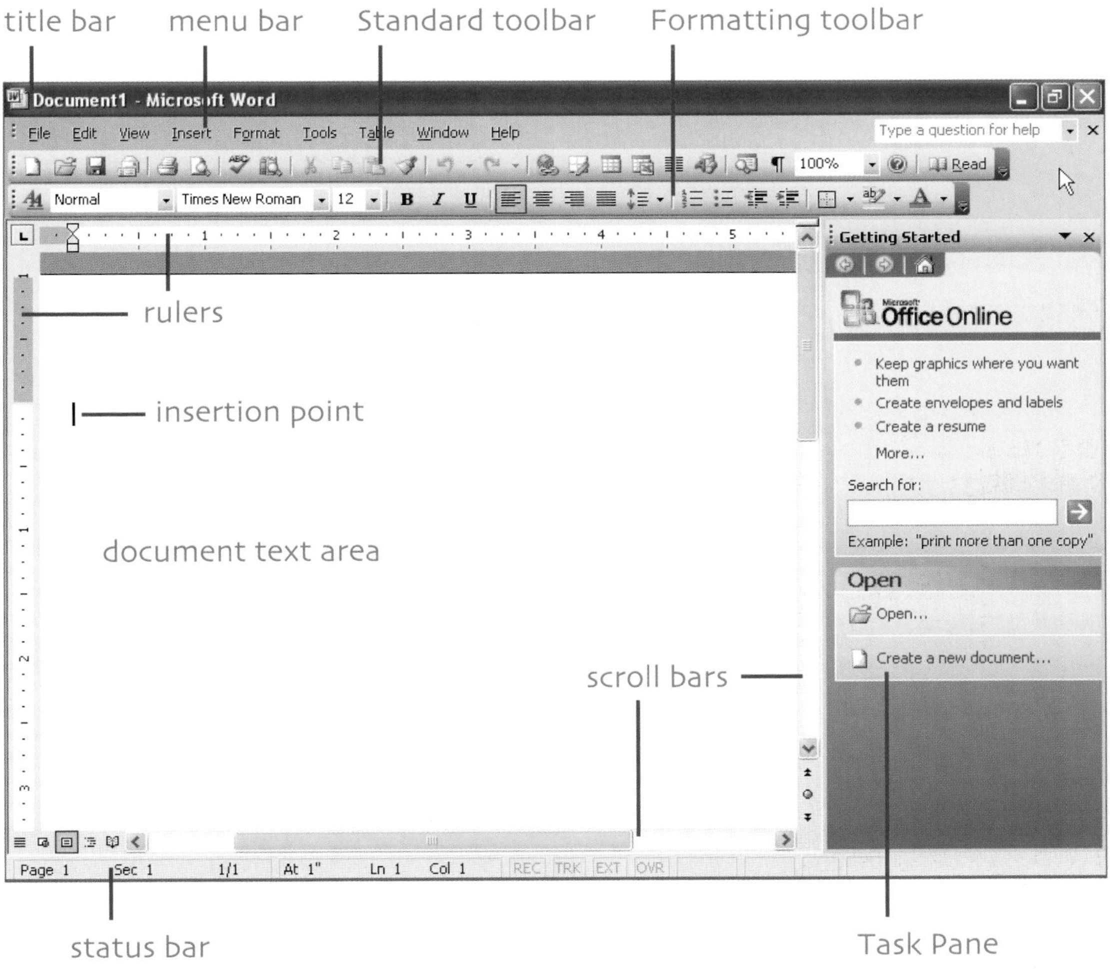

title bar   menu bar   Standard toolbar   Formatting toolbar

rulers

insertion point

document text area

scroll bars

status bar   Task Pane

look at word (Mac OS)

Here are some of the important interface elements in Word for Mac OS X.

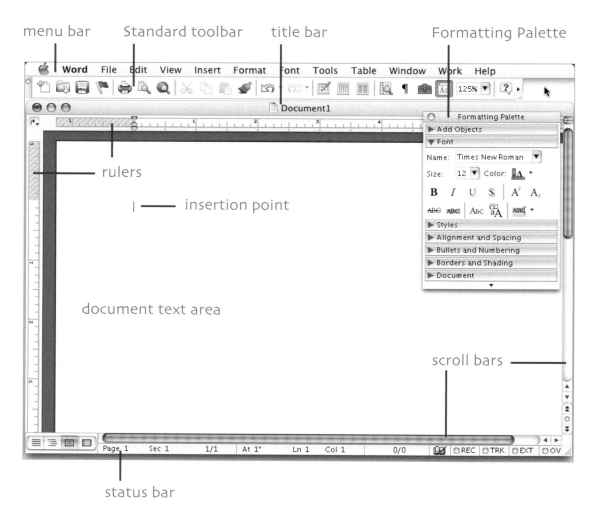

menu bar   Standard toolbar   title bar   Formatting Palette

rulers

insertion point

document text area

scroll bars

status bar

change the view

Word for Windows has five views: Normal, Web Layout, Print Layout, Reading Layout, and Outline.

Word for Mac OS has five views: Normal, Online Layout, Page Layout, Outline, and Notebook Layout.

You can change a window's view by choosing the name of the view you want from the View menu...

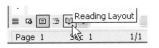

...or by clicking one of the View buttons at the bottom of the window. As shown here, you can point to a button to determine which view it's for.

Throughout this book, we'll stick to two views: Normal, and Print Layout (Windows) or Page Layout (Mac OS).

scroll a window

Scroll bars on a window make it possible to shift window contents up or down (or sideways) to see hidden contents.

A Windows
scroll bar.

A Mac OS
scroll bar.

Click the Up scroll arrow
to shift window contents
down. (Remember this:
click up to see up.)

Drag a scroll box to shift
window contents.

Click the Down scroll ar-
row to shift window con-
tents up. (Remember this:
click down to see down.)

meet microsoft word

choose from a menu

A menu is a list of commands that can be accessed from the menu bar at the top of the program window (Windows) or screen (Mac OS).

To display a menu, click its name.

To choose a menu command, click it.

A submenu is a menu that pops out of another menu when you select it.

To choose a submenu command, display the submenu and click the command.

A contextual menu appears when you right-click something (Windows) or hold down the Control key while clicking something (Mac OS).

To choose a contextual menu command, display the menu and click the command.

use a toolbar

Word has a number of toolbars with buttons you can click to access commands quickly.

In Word for Windows, two toolbars appear automatically: the Standard toolbar and the Formatting toolbar.

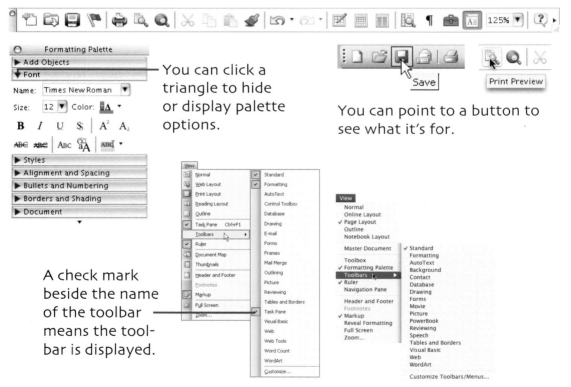

You can click a triangle to hide or display palette options.

You can point to a button to see what it's for.

A check mark beside the name of the toolbar means the toolbar is displayed.

To display a toolbar, choose its name from the Toolbars submenu under the View menu.

have a dialog

A dialog (or dialog box) is a window that appears onscreen when your computer needs to communicate with you.

When a dialog offers options for you to complete a task, it can display the options in a number of ways:

Tabs or buttons let you switch from one group of settings to another.

Scrolling lists offer multiple options in a list.

Check boxes are toggles for turning an option on or off. Click a check box to toggle its setting.

Text boxes are fields you can fill in by typing.

Drop-down lists (Windows) and pop-up menus (Mac OS) are menus within a dialog.

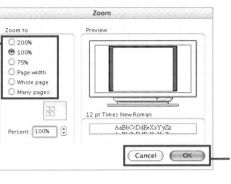

Option buttons (Windows) or radio buttons (Mac OS) let you select one option in a group.

Push buttons enable you to cancel or accept the choices in the dialog. Sometimes, push buttons can display other dialogs with other options.

exit or quit word

When you're finished using Word, you should exit or quit it.

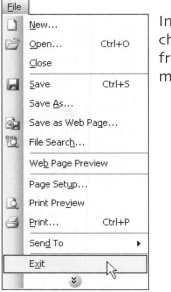

In Windows: choose Exit from the File menu.

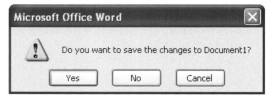

In Mac OS: choose Quit Word from the Word menu.

If a document with unsaved changes is open, Word displays a dialog that tells you and gives you a chance to save the document. (I tell you how to save documents in Chapter 2.)

extra bits

mouse around p. 3

- It is possible to get a multiple-button mouse for your Macintosh. But this book assumes you have a standard mouse with only one button.

- It's also possible to get a three-button mouse for your Windows PC. Frankly, I think two buttons are confusing enough, so I'll assume that's all your mouse has.

- You can also get a mouse with a roller—for Windows or Mac OS. (It's pretty common on Windows mice.) You can use the roller to scroll an active window. Since this feature doesn't work consistently, I don't bother talking about it in this book.

start or open word p. 4

- These instructions assume you have installed the entire Microsoft Office suite of products, including Word, Excel, PowerPoint, and Outlook (or Entourage). If you have installed just Word on your computer, consult the manual that came with it for instructions on how to start it.

- If you have a version of Word other than Word 2003 for Windows or Word 2004 for Mac OS, you might have to follow a different procedure for starting Word. Check the documentation that came with your version of Word to learn how to start it.

- Chances are, your Start menu won't look exactly like mine. But if you follow the instructions, you should be able to find and start Word using your Start menu.

- There are lots of ways to start Word in Windows and Mac OS. If you have a method you prefer, go for it!

extra bits

scroll a window p. 8

- It's possible to customize Mac OS X so the scroll arrows are at either end of the scroll bars. You do this with System Preferences. Choose System Preferences from the Apple menu and click the Appearance tab to get started. (As a long-time Mac user, I prefer them on either end; you may also.)

choose from a menu p. 9

- Contextual menus are sometimes known as shortcut menus.

- If a menu command has a shortcut key, it appears on the menu beside the command. For example, the Save command has a shortcut key of Ctrl-S (in Windows) or Command-S (in Mac OS). Pressing that key combination invokes the Save command without displaying the File menu.

use a toolbar p. 10

- In Windows, the Standard and Formatting toolbars sometimes appear on the same line. If so, not all buttons may appear. You can display the toolbars on separate lines by dragging the move handle of either toolbar down until it appears on its own line.

have a dialog p. 11

- You can select any number of check boxes in a group, but you can select only one option or radio button in a group.

2. work with a word document

As you build the documents in this project, you'll use a number of basic techniques for creating, opening, editing, formatting, and saving Word documents. Think of these techniques as a toolbox of skills that you'll use every time you work with Word.

Rather than present these skills over and over in every chapter in which they're used—which would probably waste a lot of pages and make me sound like a broken record—I've presented them just once: here, in this chapter.

If you're new to Word, please go through the practice exercises in this chapter. They explain how to work with a Word document. Throughout this book, I'll be referring to this chapter's tasks, so you can avoid a lot of page flipping if you understand its contents now, before you start building project documents.

If you've been using Word for a while, you may want to skip this chapter. Go ahead. But I recommend that you at least browse through it. You might be surprised by the tips you pick up in its pages.

create a document

Word offers a number of ways to create a new blank document. Here are a few of them.

Click the New Blank Document button on the Standard toolbar. Here's what it looks like in Windows (top) and Mac OS (bottom).

New Blank Document

New Blank Document

As you'll see throughout this book, this is the technique I personally recommend. It's quick and easy!

In Windows, choose New from the File menu...

...and then click Blank document in the New Document task pane that appears.

In Mac OS, choose New Blank Document from the File menu.

Use shortcut keys:

- In Windows, press Control-N.

- In Mac OS, press Command-N.

open a document (Windows)

You can open a saved document to work with it. From within Word, you do this with the Open dialog.

1 If the document is on a diskette, CD, or other removable media, insert it into your computer.

2 Choose Open from the File menu.

The Open dialog appears. You use this dialog to find the file you want to open.

3 Choose All Word Documents from the Files of type drop-down list.

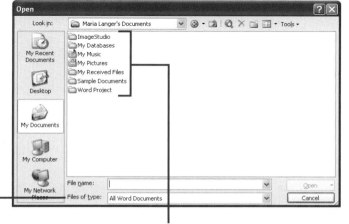

4 To look in a different disk or folder, choose the disk or folder from the Look in drop-down list.

5 To open a folder that appears in the list, double-click it. Repeat this step until you see the file you want to open.

6 Double-click the name of the file.

work with a word document   **17**

open a document (Mac OS)

You can open a saved document to work with it. From within Word, you do this with the Open dialog.

1 If the document is on a CD disc or other removable media, insert it into your computer.

2 Choose Open from the File menu.

The Open dialog appears. You use this dialog to find the file you want to open.

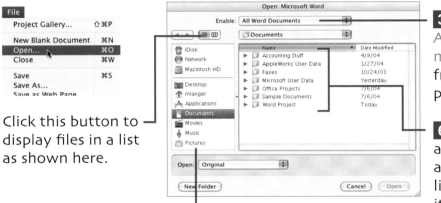

3 Make sure All Word Documents is chosen from the Enable pop-up menu.

Click this button to display files in a list as shown here.

6 To open a folder that appears in the list, double-click it. Repeat this step until you see the file you want to open.

4 To look in a different disk or folder, click the disk or folder in the Sidebar.

5 To backtrack through the file hierarchy or open a recently accessed folder, choose a location from the second pop-up menu.

7 Double-click the name of the file.

work with a word document

enter and edit text

You enter text by typing. Text appears at the blinking insertion point cursor. Create a new document and give it a try.

Here's some sample text to type. As you can see in this example, when you type too much text to fit on a line, the text automatically wraps to the next line. This is called word wrap and it's why we all threw away our typewriters.

Text automatically wraps to the next line when you've typed too much to fit on a line.

Here's some sample text to type. As you can see in this example, when you type too much text to fit on a line, the text automatically wraps to the next line. This is called word wrap and it's why we all threw away our typewriters.
I just pressed Enter (this is a Windows PC) to start a new paragraph.

Press Enter (Windows) or Return (Mac OS) at the end of a paragraph or when you want to start a new line.

If I make a misteak   If you make a mistake while typing…

If I make a mist   …you can press the Backspace key (Windows) or Delete key (Mac OS) to delete the last character(s) you typed…

If I make a mistake   …and then type the correct characters.

enter and edit text (cont'd)

Here's some sample text to type. As you can see in this example, when you type too much text to fit on a line, the text automatically wraps to the next line. This is called word wrap and it's why we all threw away our typewriters. I can also insert text anywhere in my document.

Inserted text.

I just pressed Enter (this is a Windows PC) to start a new paragraph.
If I make a mistake, I can delete the bad characters and type in good ones.

Use the arrow keys to move the blinking insertion point. This makes it easy to insert text. Just position the insertion point where you want to insert text and type.

paragraph.[
pe in good ones.|

You can also move the blinking insertion point by clicking where you want the insertion point to be. Just point...

paragraph.[[
pe in good ones.

...and click. The blinking insertion point moves. But only if you click!

select text

Selecting text is the first step to changing it. For example, you select text before you format it, copy it, or cut it. Word offers lots of ways to select text. Here are the ones I use most.

To select a single word (and any space immediately after it), double-click the word.

> Here's some sample text to type.
> much text to fit on a line, the text
> wrap and it's why we all threw av

To select any amount of text, drag over the text.

> As you can see in this example, v
> t automatically wraps to the next l
> way our typewriters. I can also in:

To select any amount of text without dragging, position the insertion point at the beginning of the text...

> |Here's some sample text to type.
> much text to fit on a line, the text
> wrap and it's why we all threw av

...and then hold down the Shift key and click at the end of the text. (This technique is known as Shift-click.)

> Here's some sample text to type.
> much text to fit on a line, the text
> wrap and it's why we all threw av

> Here's some sample text to type. As you can see in this example, when you type too
> much text to fit on a line, the text automatically wraps to the next line. This is called word
> wrap and it's why we all threw away our typewriters. I can also insert text anywhere in

To select an entire line of text, position the mouse pointer in the left margin so it turns into an arrow pointing to the upper-right. Then click.

> Here's some sample text to type. As you can see in this example, when you type too
> much text to fit on a line, the text automatically wraps to the next line. This is called word
> wrap and it's why we all threw away our typewriters. I can also insert text anywhere in
> my document.

To select an entire paragraph of text, triple-click it.

copy and paste text

When you copy text, you place a copy of it in Word's clipboard so you can paste it elsewhere—in the same document or a different document. The original text remains in the document, right where it was when you copied it.

It's easy to repeat yourself with Word.

1 Select the text you want to copy.

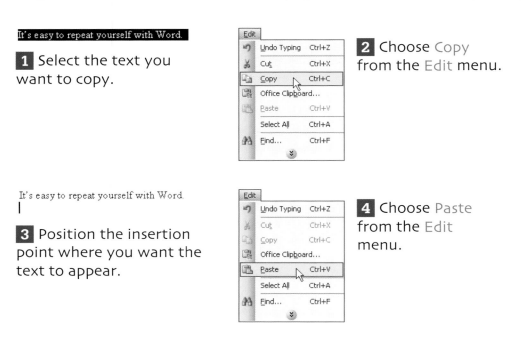

2 Choose Copy from the Edit menu.

It's easy to repeat yourself with Word.

3 Position the insertion point where you want the text to appear.

4 Choose Paste from the Edit menu.

It's easy to repeat yourself with Word.
It's easy to repeat yourself with Word.

This is a Paste Options button. See extra bits.

A copy of the text appears at the insertion point.

cut and paste text

When you cut text, you remove it from the document and place it in Word's clipboard so you can paste it elsewhere—in the same document or a different document.

1 Select the text you want to cut.

Try this: It's easy to move text with Word. Just use Cut and Paste.

Edit

Undo Typing	⌘Z
Repeat Doc Close	⌘Y
Cut	⌘X
Copy	⌘C
Copy to Scrapbook	⇧⌘C
Paste	⌘V
Paste from Scrapbook	⇧⌘V
Paste Special...	
Paste as Hyperlink	
Clear	▶
Select All	⌘A
Find...	⌘F
Replace...	⇧⌘H
Go To...	⌘G
Links...	
Object	

2 Choose Cut from the Edit menu.

Try this: |
Just use Cut and Paste.

The text disappears.

Try this:
Just use Cut and Paste.
|

3 Position the insertion point where you want the text to appear.

Edit

Undo Cut	⌘Z
Repeat Cut	⌘Y
Cut	⌘X
Copy	⌘C
Copy to Scrapbook	⇧⌘C
Paste	⌘V
Paste from Scrapbook	⇧⌘V
Paste Special...	
Paste as Hyperlink	
Clear	▶
Select All	⌘A
Find...	⌘F
Replace...	⇧⌘H
Go To...	⌘G
Links...	
Object	

4 Choose Paste from the Edit menu.

This is a Paste Options button. See extra bits.

Try this:
Just use Cut and Paste.
It's easy to move text with Word.|

The text you cut appears at the insertion point.

drag and drop

Another way to move or copy text is to drag it to a new location.

To move text:

1 Select the text you want to move.

2 Position the mouse pointer on the text. It should look like an arrow.

3 Drag the text into a new position.

> You can move text from one place to another by just dragging it. Drag and drop is a little quicker than cut and paste, but it requires a steady hand.

As you drag, an insertion point appears to indicate where the text will be moved.

4 Release the mouse button. The text appears in the new location.

> Drag and drop is a little quicker than cut and paste, but it requires a steady hand. You can move text from one place to another by just dragging it.

To copy text:

1 Select the text you want to copy.

2 Position the mouse pointer on the text. It should look like an arrow.

3 Hold down the Control key (Windows) or

> You can also copy text by dragging it. Remember to hold down the Control (Windows) or Option (Mac OS) key while dragging.

Option key (Mac OS) and drag the text into a new position. A plus sign icon appears to indicate that the text will be copied. As you drag, an insertion point also appears to indicate where the text will be copied.

4 Release the mouse button. The text is copied to the location.

> You can also copy text by dragging it. Remember to hold down the Control (Windows) or Option (Mac OS) key while dragging. You can also copy text by dragging it.

work with a word document

undo actions

Ever do something on your computer and immediately say "Oops"? (Or something a little less polite?) If so, you should know about the Undo command. Available under the Edit menu of most programs—including Word—Undo can reverse the last thing you did.

Suppose you used drag and drop to move some text and your finger slipped off the mouse button before you had the text right where you wanted it. Oops! Choose Undo from the Edit menu to put it back where it was so you can start all over again.

Word supports multiple levels of undo. That means if you made a string of mistakes, you can undo all of them. Just keep choosing that Undo command until the document is restored to the way you want it.

Edit	
↩ Undo Cut	Ctrl+Z
✂ Cut	Ctrl+X
⧉ Copy	Ctrl+C
⧉ Office Clipboard...	
⧉ Paste	Ctrl+V
Select All	Ctrl+A
🔍 Find...	Ctrl+F
⌄	

Edit	
Undo Move	⌘Z
Can't Repeat	⌘Y
Cut	⌘X
Copy	⌘C
Copy to Scrapbook	⇧⌘C
Paste	⌘V
Paste from Scrapbook	⇧⌘V
Paste Special...	
Paste as Hyperlink	
Clear	▶
Select All	⌘A
Find...	⌘F
Replace...	⇧⌘H
Go To...	⌘G
Links...	
Object	

As shown in these two screenshots, the exact wording of the Undo command varies depending on your last action.

format characters

Word has extensive formatting capabilities. The most basic formatting is font formatting, which enables you to change the appearance of text characters by applying different fonts (or typefaces), font sizes, font styles, and other effects.

One way to format text characters is with the Formatting toolbar (Windows)...

...or Formatting Palette (Mac OS).

As you can see, when you type too much text to fit on a line, the text automatically wraps to the next line. This is called word wrap and it's why we all threw away our typewriters.

1 Select the text you want to format.

2 Click a button...

...or choose a menu option to apply formatting.

As you can see, when you type too much text to fit on a line, the text automatically wraps to the next line. This is called *word wrap* and it's why we all threw away our typewriters.

Formatting is applied immediately.

format characters (cont'd)

Another way to format text characters is with the Font dialog.

1 Select the text you want to format.

2 Choose Font from the Format menu.

3 If necessary, click the Font tab (Windows) or Font button (Mac OS) in the Font dialog that appears.

4 Select a font from the Font scrolling list.

5 Select a style from the Font style scrolling list.

6 Enter a custom font size in the Size box or select a font size from the Size scrolling list.

7 Set other options as desired.

8 Click OK to save your settings.

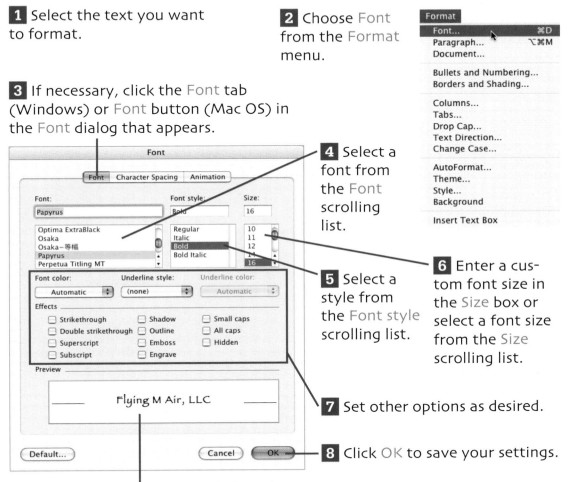

As you make changes in the dialog, the Preview area changes to show what the text will look like.

format paragraphs

Word's paragraph formatting features affect the appearance of an entire paragraph of text. Paragraph formatting includes alignment, line spacing, and indentation.

One way to format a paragraph is with the Formatting toolbar (Windows)…

...or Formatting Palette (Mac OS).

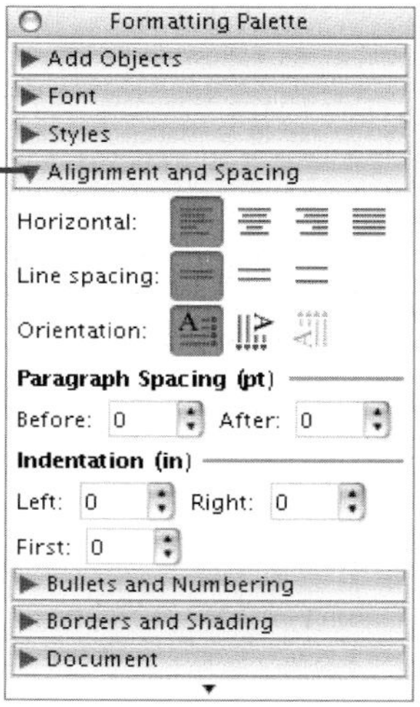

You may have to click here to display Alignment and Spacing options.

1 Select the paragraph(s) you want to format.

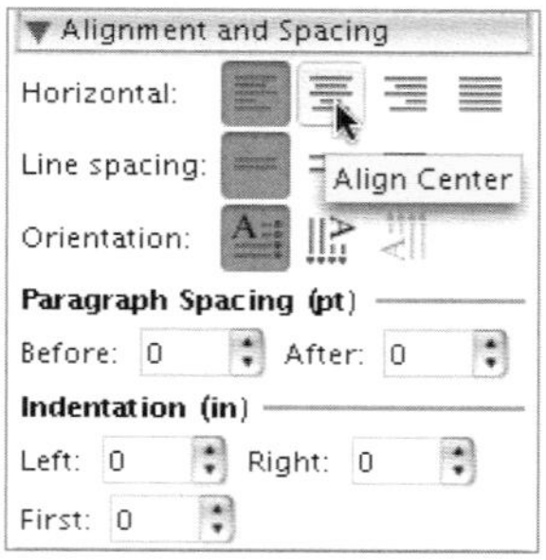

Flying M Air, LLC
12345 Main Street
Wickenburg, AZ 85390
928/555-1212

2 Click a button…

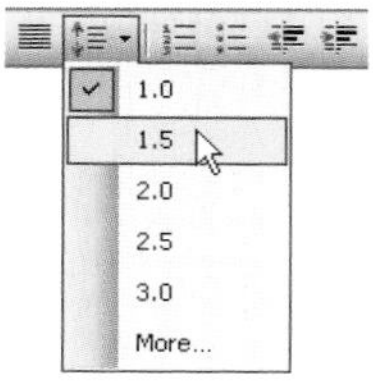

…or choose a menu option to apply formatting to the entire paragraph.

Flying M Air, LLC
12345 Main Street
Wickenburg, AZ 85390
928/555-1212

Formatting is applied immediately.

format paragraphs (cont'd)

Another way to format paragraphs is with the Paragraph dialog.

1 Select the paragraph(s) you want to format.

2 Choose Paragraph from the Format menu.

3 In the Paragraph dialog, click the Indents and Spacing tab (Windows) or Indents and Spacing button (Mac OS).

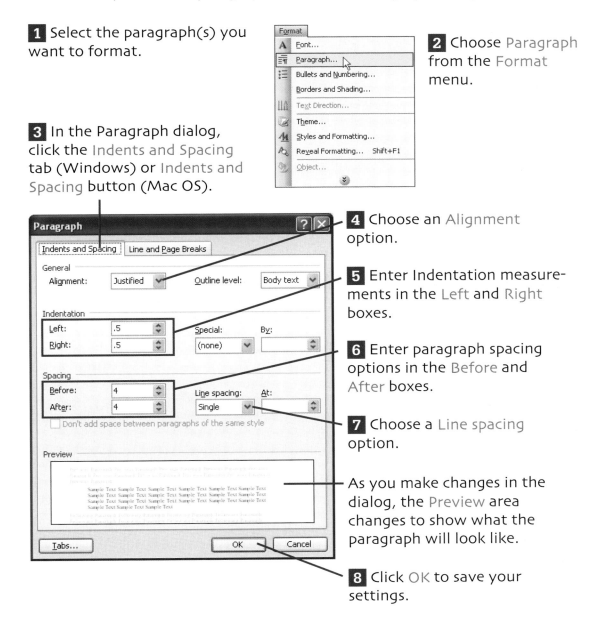

4 Choose an Alignment option.

5 Enter Indentation measurements in the Left and Right boxes.

6 Enter paragraph spacing options in the Before and After boxes.

7 Choose a Line spacing option.

As you make changes in the dialog, the Preview area changes to show what the paragraph will look like.

8 Click OK to save your settings.

print a document (Windows)

When you're finished creating a document, you can print it.

1 With the document you want to print displayed, choose Print from the File menu to display the Print dialog.

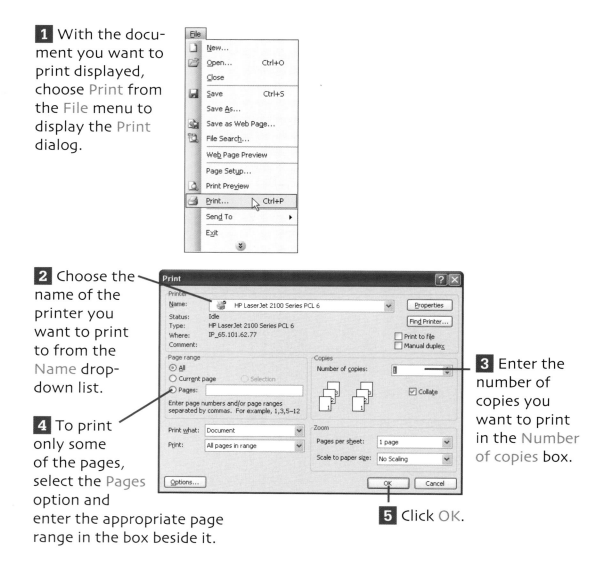

2 Choose the name of the printer you want to print to from the Name drop-down list.

4 To print only some of the pages, select the Pages option and enter the appropriate page range in the box beside it.

3 Enter the number of copies you want to print in the Number of copies box.

5 Click OK.

work with a word document

print a document (Mac OS)

When you're finished creating a document, you can print it.

1 With the document you want to print displayed, choose Print from the File menu to display the Print dialog.

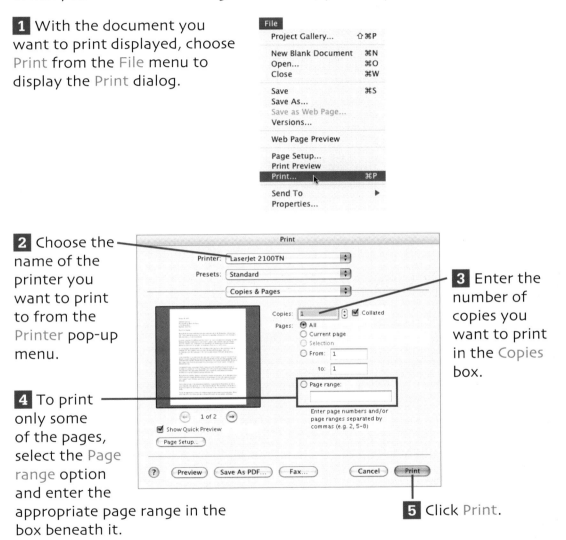

2 Choose the name of the printer you want to print to from the Printer pop-up menu.

3 Enter the number of copies you want to print in the Copies box.

4 To print only some of the pages, select the Page range option and enter the appropriate page range in the box beneath it.

5 Click Print.

save a document (Windows)

You can save a document to keep a record of it on disk or so you can open and work with it at a later date.

1 With the document you want to save displayed, choose Save from the File menu.

The Save As dialog appears. You use this dialog to navigate to the location where you want to save the file.

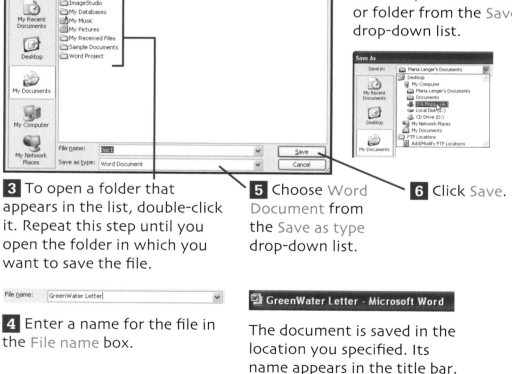

2 To open a different disk or folder, choose the disk or folder from the Save in drop-down list.

3 To open a folder that appears in the list, double-click it. Repeat this step until you open the folder in which you want to save the file.

5 Choose Word Document from the Save as type drop-down list.

6 Click Save.

4 Enter a name for the file in the File name box.

The document is saved in the location you specified. Its name appears in the title bar.

work with a word document

save a document (Mac OS)

You can save a document to keep a record of it on disk or so you can open and work with it at a later date.

1 With the document you want to save displayed, choose Save from the File menu.

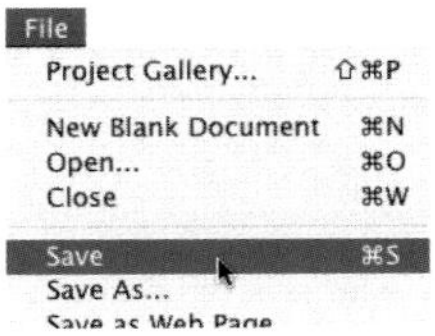

File
Project Gallery...   ⇧⌘P
New Blank Document   ⌘N
Open...   ⌘O
Close   ⌘W
Save   ⌘S
Save As...
Save as Web Page

The Save As dialog appears. You use this dialog to navigate to the location where you want to save the file.

Click this button to display files in a list as shown here.

Click this button to expand the dialog and show the file list.

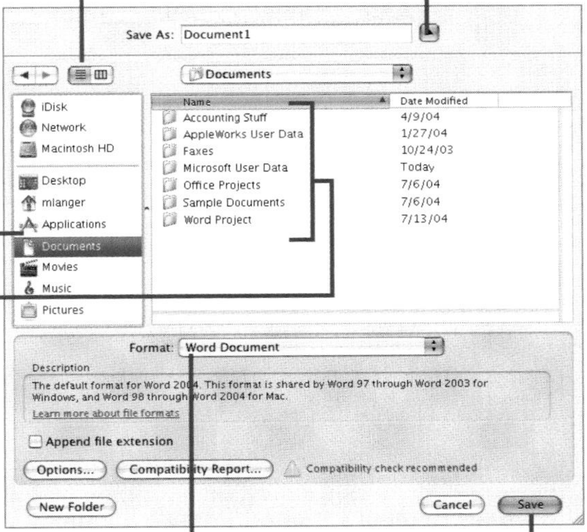

2 To open a different disk or folder, click the disk or folder in the Sidebar.

Save As: Document1

Documents

	Name	▲	Date Modified
iDisk	Accounting Stuff		4/9/04
Network	AppleWorks User Data		1/27/04
Macintosh HD	Faxes		10/24/03
Desktop	Microsoft User Data		Today
mlanger	Office Projects		7/6/04
Applications	Sample Documents		7/6/04
Documents	Word Project		7/13/04
Movies			
Music			
Pictures			

3 To backtrack through the file hierarchy or open a recently accessed folder, choose a location from the pop-up menu.

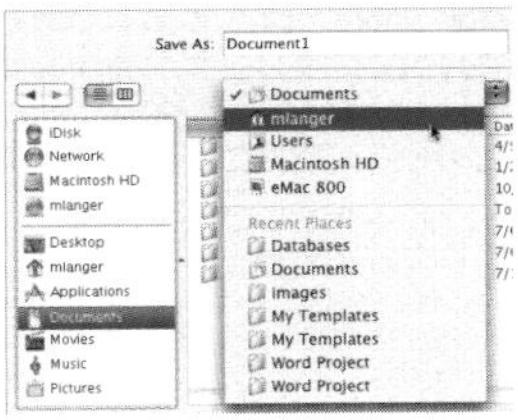

4 To open a folder that appears in the list, double-click it. Repeat this step until you open the folder in which you want to save the file.

Format: Word Document

Description
The default format for Word 2004. This format is shared by Word 97 through Word 2003 for Windows, and Word 98 through Word 2004 for Mac.
Learn more about file formats

☐ Append file extension

(Options...) (Compatibility Report...) ⚠ Compatibility check recommended

(New Folder)   (Cancel) (Save)

Save As: Document1

Documents
	mlanger
iDisk	Users
Network	Macintosh HD
Macintosh HD	eMac 800
mlanger	
Desktop	Recent Places
mlanger	Databases
Applications	Documents
Documents	Images
Movies	My Templates
Music	My Templates
Pictures	Word Project
	Word Project

6 Choose Word Document from the Format pop-up menu.

7 Click Save.

Save As: GreenWater Letter

5 Enter a name for the file in the Save As box.

⊙ ⊙ ⊙   GreenWater Letter

The document is saved in the location you specified. Its name appears in the title bar.

close a document

There are two ways to close a document.

Click the window's Close button.

Here's what it looks like in Windows…

…and here's what it looks like in Mac OS X.

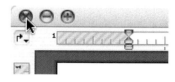

Choose Close from the File menu.

If you close a document that contains unsaved changes, a dialog like this appears in Windows (top) or Mac OS (bottom). Click a button:

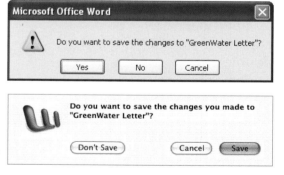

• Yes (Windows) or Save (Mac OS) saves the document. If the document has never been saved, the Save As dialog—see pages 32 and 33—appears. Follow the instructions on those pages to save the document.

• No (Windows) or Don't Save (Mac OS) closes the document without saving it. Any changes you made since it was last saved will be lost.

• Cancel tells Word not to close the document.

work with a word document

extra bits

open a document (Windows) p. 17

- You can also open a Word document from within Windows Explorer. Locate the icon for the document you want to open and double-click it.

open a document (Mac OS) p. 18

- The Sidebar appears in the Open dialog in Mac OS X 10.3 (Panther) and later only.
- You can also open a Word document from within the Finder. Locate the icon for the document you want to open and double-click it.

enter and edit text pp. 19-20

- You can delete the character immediately to the right of the insertion point by pressing the Delete key (Windows) or Del key (Mac OS).
- Pressing the Backspace key (Windows) or Delete key (Mac OS) while text is selected deletes the selected text.

- If you see black (Windows) or gray (Mac OS) dots between words and a ¶ symbol at the end of paragraphs, don't panic. This is the formatting marks (Windows) or non-printing characters (Mac OS) feature in action. The characters don't print. But if seeing them bugs you, click the Show/Hide ¶ button on the Standard toolbar and they'll go away.

Dear·Sir·or·Madam¶
¶
Flying·M·Air·has·been·conducting·helicopter·rides·and·tours·in·the·Wickenburg,·AZ·area·since·2001.·This·winter/spring·season,·we're·interested·in·expanding·our·business·to·offer·helicopter·rides·and·tours·in·a·resort·environment.¶

- As you type, you may see red or green squiggly underlines beneath certain text. Red underlines indicate potential spelling errors and green underlines indicate potential grammar errors. I explain how to resolve spelling and grammar errors in Chapter 4.

I recently visited the GreenWater and liked what I saw. I am very interested in bringing our 2004 Robinson R44 Raven helicopter to your resort to conduct rides and tours either on a regular basis (for example, every weekend or every Saturday) or in conjunction with other activities planned at your resort (for example, on weekends of boat races or ATV events).

extra bits

select text p. 21

- Word may automatically select entire words whenever you select more than just one word. If you find this feature as annoying as I do, you can turn it off. In Windows, choose Options from the Tools menu to display the Options dialog. In Mac OS, choose Preferences from the Word menu to display the Preferences dialog. Click the Edit tab (Windows) or the Edit list item (Mac OS). Then turn off the check box marked When selecting, automatically select entire word. Click OK.

copy and paste text p. 22
cut and paste text p. 23

- You can also use shortcut keys for the Copy, Cut, and Paste commands. In Windows, they are Control-C, Control-X, and Control V. In Mac OS, they are Command-C, Command-X, and Command-V.

- Word's smart cut-and-paste feature automatically adds or removes space characters when you paste text.

- The Paste Options button appears when you use the Paste command. Click this button to display a menu of options for the text you pasted.

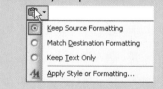

work with a word document

- If you don't want to see the Paste Options button every time you use the Paste command, you can turn off this feature. In Windows, choose Options from the Tools menu to display the Options dialog. In Mac OS, choose Preferences from the Word menu to display the Preferences dialog. Click the Edit tab (Windows) or the Edit list item (Mac OS). Then turn off the check box marked Show Paste Options buttons. Click OK to save this change.

undo actions p. 25

- You can also use a shortcut key for the Undo command: Control-Z in Windows and Command-Z in Mac OS.

- The Undo button on the Standard toolbar is really a menu. Use it to choose multiple actions to undo at once.

- If you say "Oops!" right after using the Undo command, you probably need to undo the Undo. Choose Redo from the Edit menu. If it's available, it will appear right beneath the Undo command.

extra bits

print a document pp. 30-31

- You can also use a shortcut key for the Print command: Control-P in Windows and Command-P in Mac OS.

- The instructions in this book assume you have already set up at least one printer for use with your computer. If you have not, you can learn how by checking the documentation that came with your computer or with your printer.

save a document pp. 32-33

- You can also use a shortcut key for the Save command: Control-S in Windows and Command-S in Mac OS.

- Once a document has been saved, using the Save command automatically saves it with the same name in the same location on disk as the last time you saved it. It does not display the Save As dialog again.

- If you want to save a document with a different name or in a different location on disk, use the Save As command. This command always displays the Save As dialog, so you can give the document a name and choose a save location.

close a document p. 34

- All open documents automatically close when you use the Exit (Windows) or Quit (Mac OS) command. I tell you more about exiting or quitting Word in Chapter 1.

3. create a letterhead template

Letterhead. It sounds so formal, like something a big business would use to send letters to stockholders.

But whether you're building a business from the ground up or are just using Word to handle personal writing tasks, letterhead should be one of your writing tools. At the very minimum, it provides contact information for you or your business. It can also help reinforce your company identity by displaying your logo or other brand information where it will be seen by everyone you write to.

Microsoft Word's template feature enables you to create two kinds of preformatted letterhead documents:

One kind is designed to be printed on blank paper. It includes all the text and graphics on every letter you write. Then, when you write and print the letter, the letterhead is printed as part of the letter. Here's an example. ————

The other kind is designed to be printed on preprinted letterhead. It just includes formatting settings. Then, when you write and print the letter, the body of your letter is formatted properly.

This chapter explains how to create the first kind of template.

prepare a document

1 Click the New Blank Document button on the Standard toolbar.

Here's what it looks like in Windows...

...and here's what it looks like in Mac OS X.

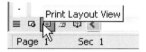

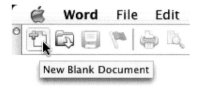

A blank document window appears.

2 Click the Print Layout View button (Windows)...

...or Page Layout View button (Mac OS) at the bottom of the window.

This switches you to a layout view where you can see exactly how each page of your document will look as you work with it.

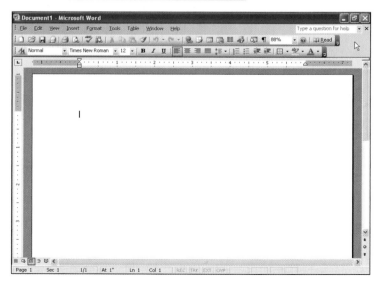

create a letterhead template

set margins

In Windows:

1 Choose Page Setup from the File menu.

File		
New...		
Open...	Ctrl+O	
Close		
Save	Ctrl+S	
Save As...		
Save as Web Page...		
File Search...		
Web Page Preview		
Page Setup...		
Print Preview		
Print...	Ctrl+P	
Send To	▶	
Exit		

In Mac OS:

1 Choose Document from the Format menu.

Format	
Font...	⌘D
Paragraph...	⌥⌘M
Document...	
Bullets and Numbering...	
Borders and Shading...	
Columns...	
Tabs...	
Drop Cap...	
Text Direction...	
Change Case...	
AutoFormat...	
Theme...	
Style...	
Background	
Object...	

2 If necessary, click the Margins tab in the Page Setup dialog that appears.

Page Setup

Margins | Paper | Layout

Margins
Top: 1"   Bottom: 1"
Left: 1.25"   Right: 1.25"
Gutter: 0"   Gutter position: Left

Orientation
Portrait   Landscape

Pages
Multiple pages: Normal

Preview
Apply to: Whole document

Default...   OK   Cancel

2 If necessary, click the Margins button in the Document dialog that appears.

Document

Margins | Layout

Top: 1"
Bottom: 1"
Left: 1.25"
Right: 1.25"
Gutter: 0"

From edge
Header: 0.5"
Footer: 0.5"

Preview

Apply to: Whole document

☐ Mirror margins

Default...   Page Setup...   Cancel   OK

create a letterhead template

set margins (cont'd)

3 Enter margin measurements in the Top, Bottom, Left, and Right boxes.

You don't have to enter the inches character; Word knows the measurement will be in inches.

Top:	.5
Bottom:	1
Left:	1
Right:	1
Gutter:	0"

Preview

As you make changes in the measurement boxes, the Preview area changes to give you an idea of what the document will look like.

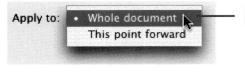

Apply to: • Whole document
This point forward

4 Make sure Whole document is selected from the Apply to menu.

5 Click OK to save your settings.

create a letterhead template

enter letterhead text

Letterhead text is the formatted text that appears at the top of every letter. You'll enter it in this step and format it in a later step.

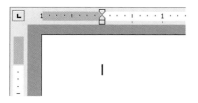

With the blinking insertion point at the top-left corner of the page…

…type in the text that you want to appear at the top of every page. Press Enter (Windows) or Return (Mac OS) after each line. For my letterhead, I want to display my company name, address, phone numbers, e-mail address, and Web site, as shown below.

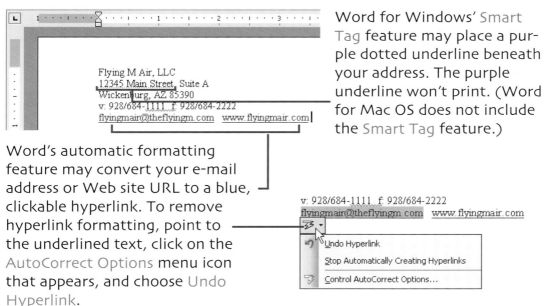

Word for Windows' Smart Tag feature may place a purple dotted underline beneath your address. The purple underline won't print. (Word for Mac OS does not include the Smart Tag feature.)

Word's automatic formatting feature may convert your e-mail address or Web site URL to a blue, clickable hyperlink. To remove hyperlink formatting, point to the underlined text, click on the AutoCorrect Options menu icon that appears, and choose Undo Hyperlink.

create placeholders

Text placeholders will help guide you when it comes time to write the letter. They also make it easy to apply consistent formatting to the body of the letter before the letter is written.

1 Make sure the blinking insertion point is at the end of the letterhead text. Then press Enter (Windows) or Return (Mac OS) twice to move it down two lines.

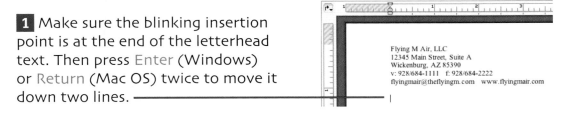

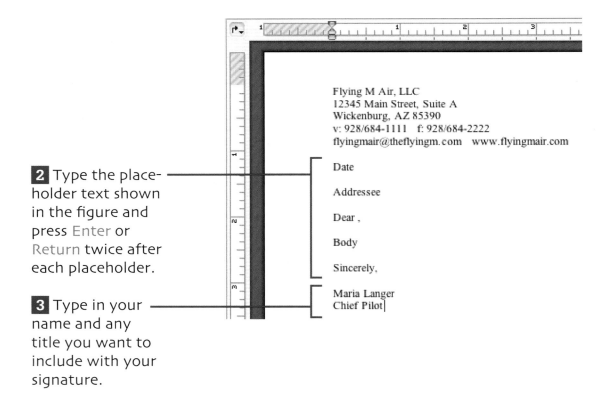

2 Type the placeholder text shown in the figure and press Enter or Return twice after each placeholder.

3 Type in your name and any title you want to include with your signature.

create a letterhead template

align text

The letterhead text will look better if centered at the top of the page.

1 Drag the mouse pointer over the letterhead text to select it.

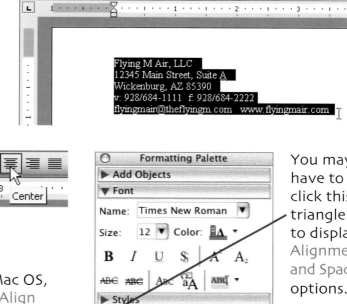

2 In Windows, click the Center button on the Formatting toolbar...

...or in Mac OS, click the Align Center button in the Alignment and Spacing area of the Formatting Palette.

You may have to click this triangle to display Alignment and Spacing options.

The selected text is centered between the margins.

apply font formatting

You can format the letterhead text so it stands out by applying font formatting. You should also format the placeholder text with a typeface that's easy to read.

1 Drag the mouse pointer over the text you want to format to select it.

2 Choose Font from the Format menu.

3 Set options in the Font screen of the Font dialog. I tell you more about using this dialog in Chapter 2.

4 Click OK.

5 Repeat this process for any letterhead or placeholder text in the document.

Format	
Font...	⌘D
Paragraph...	⌥⌘M
Document...	
Bullets and Numbering...	
Borders and Shading...	
Columns...	
Tabs...	
Drop Cap...	
Text Direction...	
Change Case...	
AutoFormat...	
Theme...	
Style...	
Background	
Insert Text Box	

Font

Font / Character Spacing / Animation

Font: Papyrus
Font style: Bold
Size: 16

Optima ExtraBlack, Osaka, Osaka—等幅, Papyrus, Perpetua Titling MT

Regular, Italic, Bold, Bold Italic

10, 11, 12, 14, 16

Font color: Automatic
Underline style: (none)
Underline color: Automatic

Effects:
- ☐ Strikethrough
- ☐ Double strikethrough
- ☐ Superscript
- ☐ Subscript
- ☐ Shadow
- ☐ Outline
- ☐ Emboss
- ☐ Engrave
- ☐ Small caps
- ☐ All caps
- ☐ Hidden

Preview

Flying M Air, LLC

Default... / Cancel / OK

Flying M Air, LLC
12345 Main Street, Suite A
Wickenburg, AZ 85390
v: 928/684-1111 f: 928/684-2222
flyingmair@theflyingm.com www.flyingmair.com

Date

Addressee

Dear ,

Body

Sincerely,

Maria Langer
Chief Pilot

Here's what my letterhead looks like with various sizes and styles of Papyrus font applied to letterhead text and Garamond font applied to placeholder text.

create a letterhead template

insert an image

Since my company uses an image as its logo, I want to place it on the letter-head, right at the top.

1 Click to the left of the first character in the letterhead text to position the blinking insertion point there.

Flying M Air, LLC
12345 Main Street, Suite A
Wickenburg, AZ 85390
v: 928/684-1111 f: 928/684-2222
flyingmair@theflyingm.com www.flyingmair.com

2 Press Enter (Windows) or Return (Mac OS) to shift the text down one line, then press the Up Arrow key once to move the insertion point up to the blank line.

Flying M Air, LLC
12345 Main Street, Suite A
Wickenburg, AZ 85390
v: 928/684-1111 f: 928/684-2222
flyingmair@theflyingm.com www.flyingmair.com

3 Choose From File from the Picture submenu under the Insert menu.

The Insert Picture (Windows) or Choose a Picture (Mac OS) dialog appears, as shown on the next page.

Insert	
Break...	
Page Numbers...	
Date and Time...	
Symbol...	
Picture ▶	Clip Art...
Hyperlink... Ctrl+K	From File...
	AutoShapes
	WordArt...
	Chart

create a letterhead template

insert an image (cont'd)

4 Use tools within the dialog to navigate to and open the folder in which the image file resides. (I explain how to use a dialog like this in Chapter 2.)

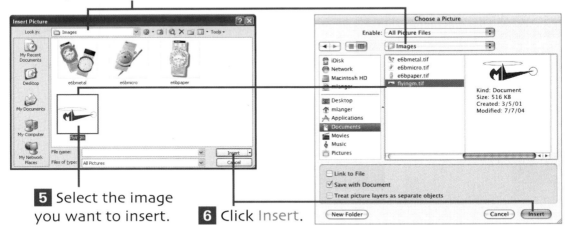

5 Select the image you want to insert.

6 Click Insert.

The image appears in the document.

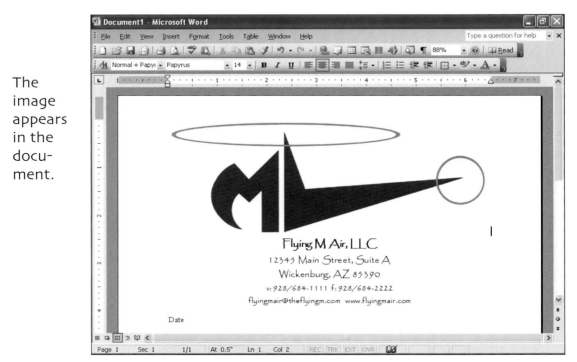

create a letterhead template

resize an image

Although I love the image that artist Gary-Paul Prince created for my company logo, I really don't want it to take up so much space on my letterhead. So I'll resize it.

1 Click the logo to select it. A box with resizing handles appears around the image.

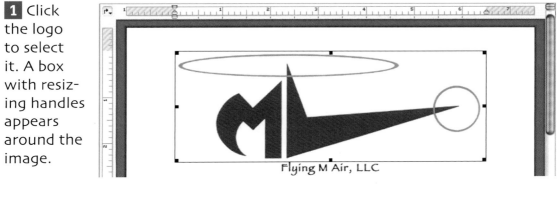

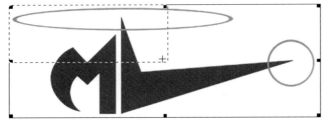

2 Position the mouse pointer on a corner resizing handle, press the mouse button down, and drag toward the middle of the image. A dotted-line box indicates the size the image will be when you release the mouse button.

3 When the image box is the size you want, release the mouse button. The image resizes.

Flying M Air, LLC
12345 Main Street, Suite A
Wickenburg, AZ 85390
v: 928/684-1111 f: 928/684-2222
flyingmair@theflyingm.com www.flyingmair.com

save as a template

When the letterhead document is just the way you want it, you can save it as a template. A template is a special type of Word document that you can use as a starting point for creating other documents.

1 Choose Save As from the File menu to display the Save As dialog.

When you save a document as a template, Word automatically displays the contents of the Templates (Windows) or My Templates (Mac OS) folder.

3 Enter Letterhead in the File name (Windows) or Save As (Mac OS) box.

2 Choose Document Template from the Save as type drop-down list (Windows) or Format pop-up menu (Mac OS).

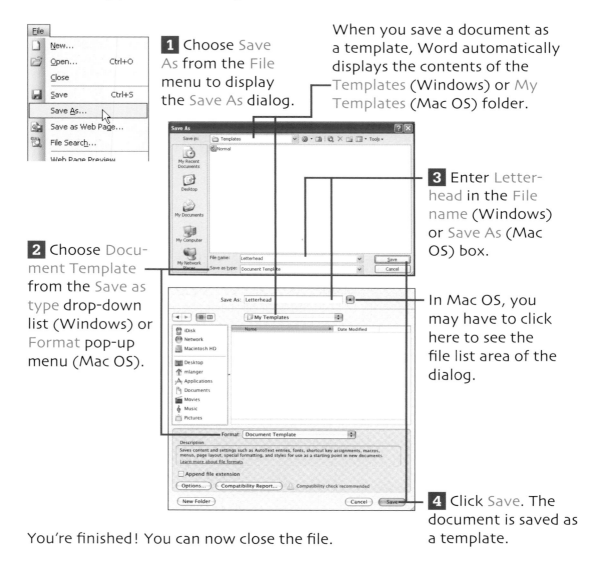

In Mac OS, you may have to click here to see the file list area of the dialog.

4 Click Save. The document is saved as a template.

You're finished! You can now close the file.

extra bits

prepare a document p. 40

- Print Layout View and Page Layout View are the same. For some reason, Microsoft gave this view different names for Windows and Mac OS.

- You can create a letterhead in any document view. Print Layout View (Windows) or Page Layout View (Mac OS) is best when working with headers and footers or positioning graphics.

set margins pp. 41-42

- If you're creating a template for use with preprinted letterhead, measure the distance from the top of the letterhead paper to the bottom of any text or graphics printed there. Then add a tiny bit—perhaps 0.1 or 0.2 inches—and use that as your top margin measurement. If there's printing on the bottom of the page, measure from the bottom of the paper to the top of the text or graphics there, add a tiny bit, and use that as your bottom margin measurement. This ensures that any letter you write with your letterhead template will not overprint preprinted text or graphics.

- The Gutter box in Margins options is for spacing on bound documents. Keep it set to 0 for single-page documents like a letterhead template.

- Clicking the Default button in the Page Setup (Windows) or Document (Mac OS) dialog enables you to establish the current settings as the default settings for all new blank documents.

enter letterhead text p. 43

- If Smart Tag underlines bother you—they drive me nuts!— point to the underlined text, click on the Smart Tag menu icon that appears, and choose Remove this Smart Tag from the menu.

- What you include in your letterhead is entirely up to you. I like to include the same information that can be found on my business card.

extra bits

create placeholders p. 44

- You don't have to create place-holder text if you don't want to.
- The main benefit of using place-holder text is that it enables you to set formatting for the text that will make up your letter.

apply font formatting p. 46

- Although applying colors to text makes it look great on screen, you'll need a color printer for the colors to appear when the letterhead is printed.
- Don't get carried away with font formatting! Although it's a lot of fun to play with fonts, sizes, and styles, too much for-matting can make a document look trashy. Limit yourself to no more than three fonts in your document. (I used only two.)
- When applying font formatting to placeholder text, be sure to choose a font that is legible. What good is a letter if the re-cipient can't read it?
- You don't have to change the formatting of placeholder text. The default Word font—New Times Roman for Windows and Times for Mac OS— is fine.

insert an image pp. 47-48

- The exact appearance of the Insert Picture (Windows) or Choose a Picture (Mac OS) dia-log varies depending on settings within the dialog. Don't panic if your dialog doesn't look exactly like the ones shown here.

resize an image p. 49

- You can also resize an image by double-clicking it and using the Size options of the Format Picture dialog that appears.

save as a template p. 50

- In Mac OS, turn on the Append file extension check box if you plan to share the template with a Word for Windows user.

4. write a letter

Once you've created a letterhead template, you can use that template to create professional-looking letters on your very own letterhead.

Here's how it works. Think of your letterhead template as a box of letterhead paper that never runs out. When you're ready to write a letter, you create a new document based on the template. (That's like pulling a sheet of letterhead paper out of the box.) You replace placeholder text with the text of your letter. (That's like typing the letter on the letterhead paper.) You take care of potential spelling and grammar errors. (That's like proofreading, but Word does a lot of the work.) Then you save, print, and close the document. (That's like making a copy of the letter and filing it where you can find it later on.)

If you've been using Word for a while, you may already create new documents based on existing ones that are similar. But using a template is much better. Why? Because it's virtually impossible to accidentally overwrite the original document with the new one.

In this chapter, you'll create a new document based on a template, replace placeholder text with your letter's text, use Word's proofing tools to fix potential errors, and finish up the document by formatting, saving, printing, and closing it.

Important Note: This chapter assumes that you have already created and saved a letterhead template as instructed in Chapter 3. If you haven't, go back to that chapter and work through the exercise there before continuing here.

create a letter (Windows)

When you create a letter from a template, you are creating a brand new Word document based on an existing template file.

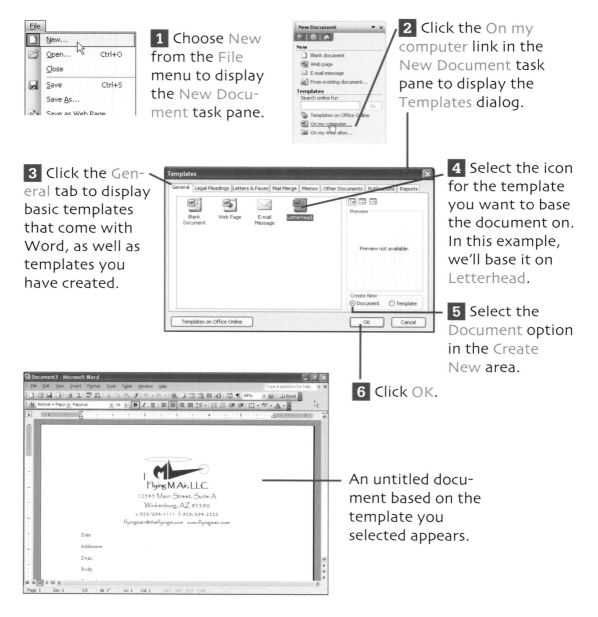

1 Choose New from the File menu to display the New Document task pane.

2 Click the On my computer link in the New Document task pane to display the Templates dialog.

3 Click the General tab to display basic templates that come with Word, as well as templates you have created.

4 Select the icon for the template you want to base the document on. In this example, we'll base it on Letterhead.

5 Select the Document option in the Create New area.

6 Click OK.

An untitled document based on the template you selected appears.

create a letter (Mac OS)

When you create a letter from a template, you are creating a brand new Word document based on an existing template file.

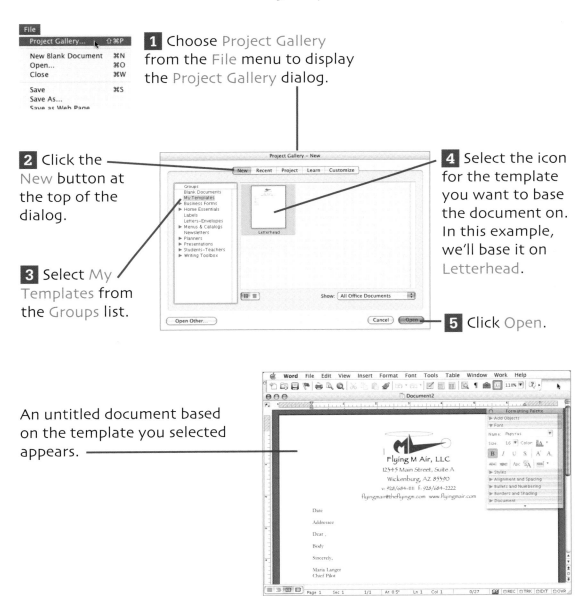

1 Choose Project Gallery from the File menu to display the Project Gallery dialog.

2 Click the New button at the top of the dialog.

3 Select My Templates from the Groups list.

4 Select the icon for the template you want to base the document on. In this example, we'll base it on Letterhead.

5 Click Open.

An untitled document based on the template you selected appears.

turn on proofing (Windows)

Word can check your spelling and grammar as you type. Although these proofing tools should be on by default, they may have been disabled. Before you start typing, you may want to confirm that they are on and ready to work.

1 Choose Options from the Tools menu to display the Options dialog.

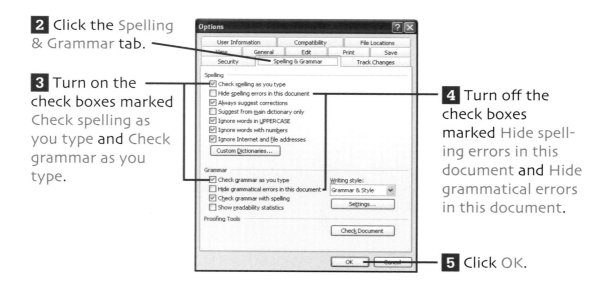

2 Click the Spelling & Grammar tab.

3 Turn on the check boxes marked Check spelling as you type and Check grammar as you type.

4 Turn off the check boxes marked Hide spelling errors in this document and Hide grammatical errors in this document.

5 Click OK.

turn on proofing (Mac OS)

Word can check your spelling and grammar as you type. Although these proofing tools should be on by default, they may have been disabled. Before you start typing, you may want to confirm that they are on and ready to work.

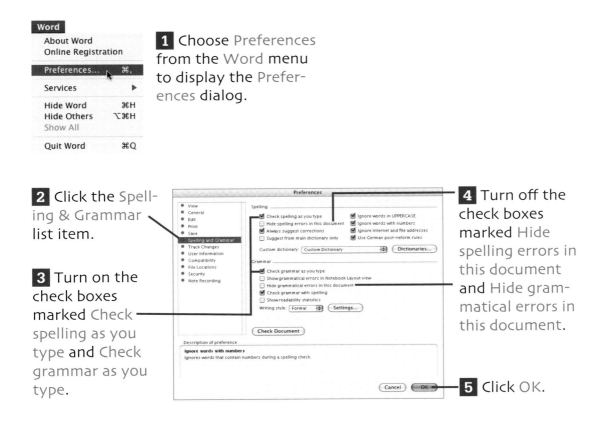

1 Choose Preferences from the Word menu to display the Preferences dialog.

2 Click the Spelling & Grammar list item.

3 Turn on the check boxes marked Check spelling as you type and Check grammar as you type.

4 Turn off the check boxes marked Hide spelling errors in this document and Hide grammatical errors in this document.

5 Click OK.

enter text

Your next task is to replace placeholder text with the text of your letter.

`Date`   **1** Double-click the word Date to select it.

October 21, 2004| **2** Type in today's date the way you want it to appear.

`Addressee`   **3** Double-click the word Addressee to select it.

John Smith
Amenities Director
The GreenWater Resort and Casino
12345 Resort Drive
Quartzsite, AZ 85344|

4 Type in the name, title, company, and address of the recipient. Be sure to press Enter (Windows) or Return (Mac OS) after each line. When you're finished, the single word should be replaced with multiple lines of text.

Dear| **5** Position the blinking insertion point immediately in front of the comma after Dear.

Dear Mr. Smith| **6** Type in the name of the person you are writing to.

`Body`   **7** Double-click the word Body to select it.

My ground crew and I will be in the Quartzsite area next Tuesday, October 26, with our new 2004 Robinson R44 Raven II helicopter and I'd like the opportunity to show you this ship and take you and one or two members of your staff for a ride and I think you'll agree that our rides would make a great activity for resort guests.

I'll be in touch later this week to confirm a time for our visit. At that time, I'll also make arrangments with you for a landing zone on the outer edges of your parking area.

I look forward to seeing you next week|

Remember, green and red squiggles under text indicate potential grammar and spelling problems. I explain how to resolve these on the next page.

8 Type in the body of your letter. Be sure to press Enter (Windows) or Return (Mac OS) at the end of each paragraph—not at the end of each line! If you need help, refer to Chapter 2.

write a letter

resolve spelling errors

If Word's proofing tools are enabled, Word may indicate potential errors as you type. Red squiggly lines under text indicate possible spelling errors or repeated words. You can use a contextual menu to resolve these errors.

1 Right-click (Windows) or hold down the Control key and click (Mac OS) on a possible spelling error to display a menu of options.

2 Choose an appropriate option from the menu.

Add to Dictionary (Windows) or Add (Mac OS) tells Word to add the word to your dictionary so it knows it for the future. The red squiggles disappear and Word will never mark the word as a possible error again.

Here's an example of a contextual menu full of options for a possible spelling error in Windows.

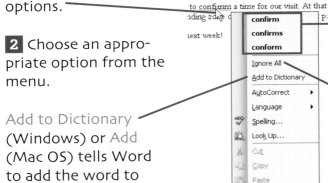

Possible corrections are listed at the top of the menu. Choose a correction to replace the marked word.

Ignore All tells Word to ignore all occurrences of the word in this document. The red squiggles disappear.

resolve grammar errors

Green squiggly lines under text indicate possible grammar or style errors. You can also use a contextual menu to learn more about and resolve these errors.

1 Right-click (Windows) or hold down the Control key and click (Mac OS) on a possible grammar error to display a menu of options.

2 Choose an appropriate option from the menu.

Ignore Once (Windows) or Ignore (Mac OS) tells Word to ignore this potential problem. This removes the green squiggles.

Here are two examples of contextual menus full of options for possible grammar errors in Mac OS.

At that time, I'll also make your parking are

Help
I will
Ignore
About this Sentence
Grammar...

Possible replacement text appears near the top of the menu. Choose a correction to replace the marked word or phrase.

My ground crew and I will be in the Quartzsite area next Tuesday, October 26, with our new 2004 Robinson R44 Raven II helicopter, and I'd like the opportunity to show you this ship and take you and one or two members of your staff for a ride and I think you'll agree that our rides would make a great activity for resort guests.

I'll be in touch later this week arrangements with you for a lan

I look forward to seeing you n

Sincerely,

Maria Langer
Chief Pilot

Help
Long Sentence (consider revising)
Ignore
About this Sentence
Grammar...

A brief description of the problem with advice on how to fix it may appear in gray. You cannot choose this item. Instead, use it as guidance for fixing the problem.

Here's what the letter's text might look like once the errors have been resolved. I manually rewrote the first paragraph to break it into three separate sentences.

October 21, 2004

John Smith
Amenities Director
The GreenWater Resort & Casino
12345 Resort Drive
Quartzite, AZ 85344

Dear Mr. Smith,

My ground crew and I will be in the Quartzsite area next Tuesday, October 26, with our new 2004 Robinson R44 Raven II helicopter. I'd like the opportunity to show you this ship and take you and one or two members of your staff for a ride. I think you'll agree that our rides would make a great activity for resort guests.

I'll be in touch later this week to confirm a time for our visit. At that time, I'll also make arrangements with you for a landing zone on the outer edges of your parking area.

I look forward to seeing you next week!

Sincerely,

Maria Langer
Chief Pilot

finish up

Once you're satisfied with the content of your letter, it's time to finish up. For more information, consult Chapter 2.

1 Apply formatting. There shouldn't be much

*My ground crew and I will be in the Quartzsite area next Tuesday, October 26, with our **new 2004 Robinson R44 Raven II helicopter**. I'd like the opportunity to show you this ship and take you and one or two members of your staff for a ride. I think you'll agree that our rides would make a great activity for resort guests.*

need for this, since you've already formatted both the letterhead text and the placeholder text. But there may be some words or phrases that you want to underline, boldface, or italicize for emphasis.

2 Save the letter. When you use the Save command, Word displays the Save As dialog, just as if you'd started with a blank new document. This makes it virtually impossible to accidentally overwrite the existing template file. Be sure to save the document in your My Documents (Windows) or Documents (Mac OS) folder or some other location where you can easily find it.

3 Print the letter. If you're ready to send the letter, print out a copy to send. Don't forget to sign it before you send it out!

4 Close the document. If you're done working with the letter, you can close it.

extra bits

create a letter pp. 54-55

There is an important difference between creating a document from a template and simply opening a template:

- When you create a document from a template, you make a copy of the template that can be saved as a regular Word document.

- When you open a template, however, you open the original template and any changes you make will be saved in the template.

turn on proofing pp. 56-57

- You don't have to use both the spelling and grammar checkers. I personally don't like Word's grammar checker and normally keep it turned off when creating my documents.

- Word's AutoCorrect feature may automatically correct some spelling and typographical errors as you type. AutoCorrect is an advanced feature of Word that is not covered in this book.

enter text p. 58

- To include blank lines between paragraphs in the body of your letter, just press Enter (Windows) or Return (Mac OS) twice after each paragraph.

resolve spelling and grammar errors pp. 59-60

- Not all words and phrases that Word marks as possible spelling or grammar errors are errors. Word marks words it does not recognize as spelling errors and it marks phrases that do not meet requirements of built-in grammar and style rules as grammar errors.

- Do not add a word to Word's dictionary unless you know for sure that it is spelled correctly. Once a word is added to the dictionary, Word will never mark it as a potential error again.

- If you duplicated my letter but don't see the same green squiggles, it may be because of Writing style options set for the grammar checker. Open the Options or Preferences dialog as instructed on page 56 or 57 and make sure your settings are identical to mine.

finish up p. 61

- Don't get carried away with formatting text in the body of your letter. Too many font style changes can quickly turn a professional-looking document into something that looks very amateurish.

- Give your files descriptive names. For example, I like to name letters with the last name of the addressee followed by the date. Then I know at a glance that the document named Smith-102104 is a letter I wrote to Mr. Smith on October 21, 2004.

5. prepare a résumé

A résumé is probably the most important document you create when you're looking for a new job. This piece of paper is a concise summary of your qualifications and work experience. Like an advertisement for your capabilities, its purpose is to begin convincing the reader that you might be the right candidate for an open position. If properly prepared—and sent to the right person—it can help you get a job interview. Then it's up to you to finish what the résumé started.

In this chapter, we'll create a basic résumé with the kinds of standard formatting you'd find in most résumé documents. To help ensure consistent formatting, we'll use Word's Format Painter feature. Even if the résumé you want to create looks a bit different from this one, you should learn everything you need to know to create a résumé to your specifications.

MARIA LANGER
12345 Main Street, Suite A
Wickenburg, AZ 85390
v. 928/684-1111 f. 928/684-2222
maria@theflyingm.com

OBJECTIVE
To obtain work as a helicopter tour/charter pilot and/or Robinson helicopter ferry pilot.

QUALIFICATIONS
- Over 1,000 helicopter hours as pilot in command
- Extensive flight time in Robinson R22, Robinson R44, and Bell 206L1 helicopters
- Numerous cross-country flights in excess of 300 miles
- All Robinson Helicopter Company requirements for ferrying R22 and R44 helicopters in the southwestern United States.

EMPLOYMENT HISTORY

Papillon Airways, Grand Canyon, AZ   April 2004 to Present
Pilot/Captain
I fly Bell 206L1-C30P helicopters on tours of Grand Canyon in a variety of challenging conditions. As Captain, I have direct responsibility for the operation of my assigned aircraft and the safety of my passengers.

Flying M Air, LLC, Wickenburg, AZ   October 2001 to Present
Owner/Pilot
I fly Robinson R22 and Robinson R44 helicopters on part 91 tours of the Wickenburg area. As owner/operator of the company, I am responsible for all aspects of the business, including finances, maintenance arrangements, regulation compliance, and day-to-day operations.

Flying M Productions, Wickenburg, AZ   May 1990 to Present
Freelance Writer
I am the author of over 50 technical books and over 100 articles for computer magazines. I have also written about helicopters and aviation for Sport Aviation, SW Aviator, and America's Flyways.

Automatic Data Processing, Roseland, NJ   August 1987 to May 1990
Senior Financial Analyst
Worked on special projects to help management analyze business performance and trends. Created automated analysis applications with Lotus 1-2-3.

New York City Comptroller's Office, New York, NY   July 1982 to August 1987
Field Audit Supervisor
Worked my way up from starting position as an auditor to supervisor in less than two years. Supervised a staff of 13 auditors working throughout New York City.

EDUCATION

Papillon Airways, Grand Canyon, AZ   April 2004
Turbine Transition Training for Bell 206L1-C30P

Robinson Helicopter Company, Torrance, CA   October 2002
Factory Safety Course

Hofstra University, Hempstead, NY   September 1978 to May 1982
BBA with Highest Honors in Accounting

create a document

There are two ways to create a new document for a résumé.

If you have already created a letterhead template, as discussed in Chapter 3, you can use that as your starting document. Follow the instructions on page 54 or 55 to create a new document based on that template. Then select all the placeholder text and press Backspace (Windows) or Delete (Mac OS) to delete it. If your letterhead includes a logo and you want to exclude it from the résumé, click the logo to select it and press Backspace (Windows) or Delete (Mac OS).

If you don't want to use your letterhead—perhaps you want a more personal touch—you can follow the instructions on pages 40–43 to create a blank new document and enter your contact information at the top of the page. Then use techniques in Chapter 2 to format this information.

When you're finished, you should have a new document with just your contact information at the top of the page, like this. This example uses the Gill Sans font in various sizes. I applied bold and small caps font formatting to my name to make it stand out.

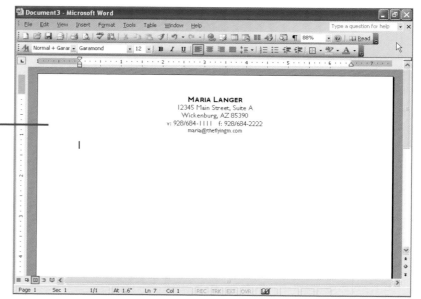

enter objective

This résumé starts with an Objective—what you want to achieve.

1 Position the insertion point on the second blank line. ————————

> **MARIA LANGER**
> 12345 Main Street, Suite A
> Wickenburg, AZ 85390
> v: 928/684-1111   f: 928/684-2222
> maria@theflyingm.com
>
> |

2 Type Objective. ——————————

> **MARIA LANGER**
> 12345 Main Street, Suite A
> Wickenburg, AZ 85390
> v: 928/684-1111   f: 928/684-2222
> maria@theflyingm.com
>
> Objective|

3 Press Enter (Windows) or Return (Mac OS).

4 Type the text of your objective.

5 Press Enter (Windows) or Return (Mac OS).

Here's what the Objective section might look like when you're done.

> **MARIA LANGER**
> 12345 Main Street, Suite A
> Wickenburg, AZ 85390
> v: 928/684-1111   f: 928/684-2222
> maria@theflyingm.com
>
> Objective
> To obtain work as a helicopter tour/charter pilot and/or Robinson helicopter ferry pilot.
> |

prepare a résumé

enter qualifications

The Qualifications section lists a few of the most important qualifications you have for the job. You can enter this information in narrative form (a paragraph) or as a list. In this example, we'll enter a list.

1 Position the insertion point on the first blank line after the Objective section. ─────────────

Objective
To obtain work as a helicopter tour/charter pilot and/or Robinson helicopter ferry pilot.

2 Type Qualifications.

3 Press Enter (Windows) or Return (Mac OS). ─────────────

Objective
To obtain work as a helicopter tour/charter pilot and/or Robinson helicopter ferry pilot.
Qualifications

4 Click the Bullets button on the Formatting toolbar (Windows; left) or the Bullets button in the Bullets and Numbering section of the Formatting Palette (Mac OS; right).

A bullet automatically appears at the beginning of the line.

Objective
To obtain work as a helicopter tour/charter pilot and/or Robinson helicopter ferry pilot.
Qualifications
•

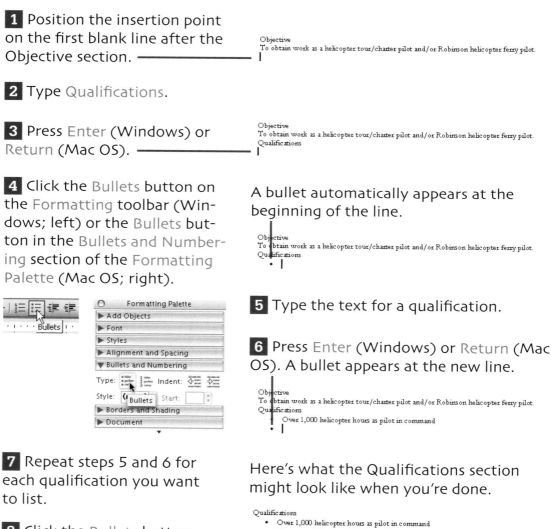

5 Type the text for a qualification.

6 Press Enter (Windows) or Return (Mac OS). A bullet appears at the new line.

Objective
To obtain work as a helicopter tour/charter pilot and/or Robinson helicopter ferry pilot.
Qualifications
        Over 1,000 helicopter hours as pilot in command
•

7 Repeat steps 5 and 6 for each qualification you want to list.

Here's what the Qualifications section might look like when you're done.

Qualifications
• Over 1,000 helicopter hours as pilot in command
• Extensive flight time in Robinson R22, Robinson R44, and Bell 206L1 helicopters
• Numerous cross-country flights in excess of 300 miles
• All Robinson Helicopter Company requirements for ferrying R22 and R44 helicopters in southwestern United States

8 Click the Bullets button again to "turn off" bullet formatting.

prepare a résumé

enter job history

The Employment History section lists your most recent or pertinent jobs, including company name, dates of employment, job title, and responsibilities.

1 Position the insertion point on the first blank line after the Qualifications section.

2 Type Employment History.

3 Press Enter (Windows) or Return (Mac OS).

Employment History

4 Type the name of the company you worked for, followed by the city and state the company is in.

5 Press the Tab key.

6 Type the dates you worked for that company.

Employment History
Papillon Airways, Grand Canyon, AZ April 2004 to Present

7 Press Enter (Windows) or Return (Mac OS).

8 Type your job title.

9 Press Enter (Windows) or Return (Mac OS).

10 Type two or three sentences describing your responsibilities in that position.

Employment History
Papillon Airways, Grand Canyon, AZ April 2004 to Present
Pilot/Captain
I fly Bell 206L1-C30P helicopters on tours of Grand Canyon in a variety of challenging conditions. As Captain, I have direct responsibility for the operation of my assigned aircraft and the safety of my passengers.

11 Press Enter (Windows) or Return (Mac OS).

12 Repeat steps 4–11 for each job you want to list.

Here's what the Employment History section might look like when you're done.

Employment History
Papillon Airways, Grand Canyon, AZ April 2004 to Present
Pilot/Captain
I fly Bell 206L1-C30P helicopters on tours of Grand Canyon in a variety of challenging conditions. As Captain, I have direct responsibility for the operation of my assigned aircraft and the safety of my passengers.
Flying M Air, LLC, Wickenburg, AZ October 2001 to Present
Owner/Pilot
I fly Robinson R22 and Robinson R44 helicopters on Part 91 tours of the Wickenburg area. As owner/operator of the company, I am responsible for all aspects of the business, including finances, maintenance arrangements, regulation compliance, and day-to-day operations.
Flying M Productions, Wickenburg, AZ   May 1990 to Present
Freelance Writer
I am the author of over 50 technical books and over 100 articles for computer magazines. I have also written about helicopters and aviation for Sport Aviation, SW Aviator, and America's Flyways.
Automatic Data Processing, Roseland, NJ   August 1987 to May 1990
Senior Financial Analyst
Worked on special projects to help management analyze business performance and trends. Created automated analysis applications with Lotus 1-2-3.
New York City Comptroller's Office, New York, NY July 1982 to August 1987
Field Audit Supervisor
Worked my way up from starting position as auditor to supervisor in less than two years. Supervised staff of 13 auditors working throughout New York City.

enter education

The Education section lists college degrees as well as pertinent training.

1 Position the insertion point on the first blank line after the Employment History section.

2 Type Education.

3 Press Enter (Windows) or Return (Mac OS).

4 Type the name of the school you went to, followed by the city and state the school is in.

5 Press the Tab key.

6 Type the dates you attended school or training.

7 Press Enter (Windows) or Return (Mac OS).

8 Type your degree or the course of study.

9 Press Enter (Windows) or Return (Mac OS).

10 Repeat steps 4–9 for each education item you want to list.

Here's what the Education section might look like when you're done.

Education
Papillon Airways, Grand Canyon, AZ April 2004
Turbine Transition Training for Bell 206L1-C30P
Robinson Helicopter Company, Torrance, CA October 2002
Factory Safety Course
Hofstra University, Hempstead, NY   September 1978 to May 1982
BBA with Highest Honors in Accounting

format headings

We'll make the headings stand out with font and paragraph formatting. We'll use the Format Painter feature to copy formatting options quickly and ensure consistency.

1 Select the first heading (Objective).

2 Choose Font from the Format menu to display the Font dialog.

3 If necessary, click the Font tab (Windows) or button (Mac OS).

4 Set formatting options as follows:
Font: Gill Sans MT or Gill Sans
Font style: Bold
Size: 14
Effects: Small caps

5 Click OK.

Your settings are applied to the selected text.

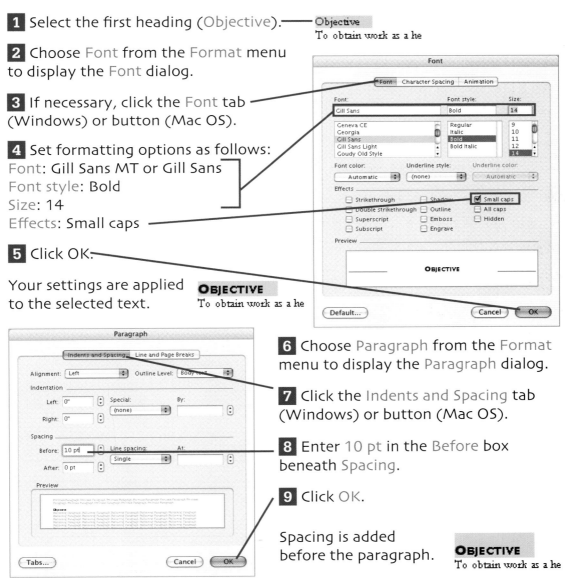

6 Choose Paragraph from the Format menu to display the Paragraph dialog.

7 Click the Indents and Spacing tab (Windows) or button (Mac OS).

8 Enter 10 pt in the Before box beneath Spacing.

9 Click OK.

Spacing is added before the paragraph.

format headings (cont'd)

10 Double-click the Format Painter button on the Standard toolbar.

Windows

Mac OS

The button becomes selected and the mouse pointer turns into a Format Painter pointer.

In Windows, the Format Painter pointer has a tiny paintbrush. 🖌

In Mac OS, the Format Painter pointer has a plus sign. ⁺

11 Select the word Qualifications. Its formatting changes to match Objective.

OBJECTIVE
To obtain work as a helicopt

QUALIFICATIONS
• Over 1,000 helicopt

12 Select the remaining headings, one at a time: Employment History and Education. The formatting of both headings changes.

13 Press Esc to turn off the Format Painter feature.

When you're finished, the résumé should look something like this.

MARIA LANGER
12345 Main Street, Suite A
Wickenburg AZ 85390
v: 928/684-1111   f: 928/684-2222
maria@theflyingm.com

OBJECTIVE
To obtain work as a helicopter tour/charter pilot and/or Robinson helicopter ferry pilot

QUALIFICATIONS
• Over 1,000 helicopter hours as pilot in command
• Extensive flight time in Robinson R22, Robinson R44, and Bell 206L1 helicopters
• Numerous cross-country flights in excess of 300 miles
• All Robinson Helicopter Company requirements for ferrying R22 and R44 helicopters in the southwestern United States.

EMPLOYMENT HISTORY
Papillon Airways, Grand Canyon, AZ April 2004 to Present
Pilot/Captain
I fly Bell 206L1-C30P helicopters on tours of Grand Canyon in a variety of challenging conditions. As Captain, I have direct responsibility for the operation of my assigned aircraft and the safety of my passengers.
Flying M Air, LLC, Wickenburg, AZ October 2001 to Present
Owner/Pilot
I fly Robinson R22 and Robinson R44 helicopters on part 91 tours of the Wickenburg area. As owner/operator of the company, I am responsible for all aspects of the business, including finances, maintenance arrangements, regulation compliance, and day-to-day operations.
Flying M Productions, Wickenburg, AZ   May 1990 to Present
Freelance Writer
I am the author of over 50 technical books and over 100 articles for computer magazines. I have also written about helicopters and aviation for Sport Aviation, SW Aviator, and America's Flyways.
Automatic Data Processing, Roseland, NJ   August 1987 to May 1990
Senior Financial Analyst
Worked on special projects to help management analyze business performance and trends. Created automated analysis applications with Lotus 1-2-3.
New York City Comptroller's Office, New York, NY July 1982 to August 1987
Field Audit Supervisor
Worked my way up from starting position as an auditor to supervisor in less than two years. Supervised a staff of 13 auditors working throughout New York City.

EDUCATION
Papillon Airways, Grand Canyon, AZ April 2004
Turbine Transition Training for Bell 206L1-C30P
Robinson Helicopter Company, Torrance, CA October 2002
Factory Safety Course
Hofstra University, Hempstead, NY   September 1978 to May 1982
BBA with Highest Honors in Accounting

prepare a résumé

format items

Now, we'll use paragraph and tab formatting for the first line of each item under Employment History and Education. The Format Painter feature will make duplicating the formatting easy.

1 Select the first line under Employment History.

EMPLOYMENT HISTORY
Papillon Airways, Grand Canyon, AZ April 2004 to Present
Pilot/Captain
I fly Bell 206L1-C30P helicopters on tours of Grand Canyon in a variety of challenging conditions.

2 Choose Paragraph from the Format menu to display the Paragraph dialog.

3 Click the Indents and Spacing tab (Windows) or button (Mac OS).

4 Type 4 pt in the Before box beneath Spacing.

5 Click Tabs to display the Tabs dialog.

6 Type 6 in the Tab stop position box.

Paragraph

Indents and Spacing | Line and Page Breaks

General
Alignment: Left   Outline level: Body text

Indentation
Left: 0"   Special: (none)   By:
Right: 0"

Spacing
Before: 4 pt   Line spacing: Single   At:
After: 0 pt
☐ Don't add space between paragraphs of the same style

Preview

Tabs...   OK   Cancel

Tabs

Tab stop position:
6

Default tab stops:
0.5"

Tab stops to be cleared:

Alignment
○ Left   ○ Center   ⦿ Right
○ Decimal   ○ Bar

Leader
⦿ 1 None   ○ 2 ....   ○ 3 -------
○ 4 ____

Set   Clear   Clear All

OK   Cancel

7 Select the Right option.

8 Click Set.

The right-aligned tab stop you created is added to the list beneath the Tab stop position box.

Tab stop position:
6"

9 Click OK to save your settings.

format items (cont'd)

The text is shifted down and a right-aligned tab stop shifts the dates to the right.

EMPLOYMENT HISTORY

Papillon Airways, Grand Canyon, AZ   April 2004 to Present
Pilot/Captain
I fly Bell 206L1-C30P helicopters on tours of Grand Canyon in a variety of challenging conditions.

10 Double-click the Format Painter button (see page 72). The mouse pointer turns into a Format Painter pointer.

11 One by one, select each paragraph containing the name of a company under Employment History. The paragraph formatting changes to match the first company.

12 One by one, select each paragraph containing the name of a school or training organization under Education. The paragraph formatting changes to match the companies.

13 Press Esc to turn off the Format Painter feature.

When you're finished, the résumé should look something like this.

MARIA LANGER
12345 Main Street, Suite A
Wickenburg AZ 85390
v: 928/684-1111   f: 928/684-2222
maria@theflyingm.com

OBJECTIVE
To obtain work as a helicopter tour/charter pilot and/or Robinson helicopter ferry pilot

QUALIFICATIONS
- Over 1,000 helicopter hours as pilot in command
- Extensive flight time in Robinson R22, Robinson R44, and Bell 206L1 helicopters
- Numerous cross-country flights in excess of 300 miles
- All Robinson Helicopter Company requirements for ferrying R22 and R44 helicopters in the southwestern United States.

EMPLOYMENT HISTORY
Papillon Airways, Grand Canyon, AZ   April 2004 to Present
Pilot/Captain
I fly Bell 206L1-C30P helicopters on tours of Grand Canyon in a variety of challenging conditions. As Captain, I have direct responsibility for the operation of my assigned aircraft and the safety of my passengers.
Flying M Air, LLC, Wickenburg, AZ   October 2001 to Present
Owner/Pilot
I fly Robinson R22 and Robinson R44 helicopters on part 91 tours of the Wickenburg area. As owner/operator of the company, I am responsible for all aspects of the business, including finances, maintenance arrangements, regulation compliance, and day-to-day operations.
Flying M Productions, Wickenburg, AZ   May 1990 to Present
Freelance Writer
I am the author of over 50 technical books and over 100 articles for computer magazines. I have also written about helicopters and aviation for Sport Aviation, SW Aviator, and America's Flyways.
Automatic Data Processing, Roseland, NJ   August 1987 to May 1990
Senior Financial Analyst
Worked on special projects to help management analyze business performance and trends. Created automated analysis applications with Lotus 1-2-3.
New York City Comptroller's Office, New York, NY   July 1982 to August 1987
Field Audit Supervisor
Worked my way up from starting position as an auditor to supervisor in less than two years. Supervised a staff of 13 auditors working throughout New York City.

EDUCATION
Papillon Airways, Grand Canyon, AZ   April 2004
Turbine Transition Training for Bell 206L1-C30P
Robinson Helicopter Company, Torrance, CA   October 2002
Factory Safety Course
Hofstra University, Hempstead, NY   September 1978 to May 1982
BBA with Highest Honors in Accounting

prepare a résumé

indent descriptions

We'll indent the descriptive text in the Employment History area using the ruler and the Format Painter.

1 Click to position the blinking insertion point anywhere in the paragraph of descriptive text under the first job's title.

> Papillon Airways, Grand Canyon, AZ   April 2004 to Present
> Pilot/Captain
> I fly Bell 206L1-C30P helicopters on tours of Grand Canyon in a variety of challenging conditions. As Captain, I have direct responsibility for the operation of my assigned aircraft and the safety of my passengers.

2 Drag the left indent marker (the bottom-most of the three left indentation markers on the ruler) about 1/4 inch to the right.

> Papillon Airways, Grand Canyon, AZ
> Pilot/Captain
> I fly Bell 206L1-C30P helicopters on to
> As Captain, I have direct responsibility
> passengers.

As you drag, a vertical line appears to indicate where the new indentation setting will appear.

When you release the mouse button, each line in the paragraph shifts to the right.

> Papillon Airways, Grand Canyon, AZ   April 2004 to Present
> Pilot/Captain
> I fly Bell 206L1-C30P helicopters on tours of Grand Canyon in a variety of challenging conditions. As Captain, I have direct responsibility for the operation of my assigned aircraft and the safety of my passengers.

3 Double-click the Format Painter button (see page 72).

4 One by one, click in each paragraph of descriptive text under your job titles. Each paragraph shifts to match the one you formatted first.

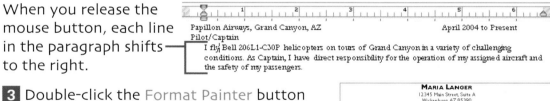

When you're finished indenting paragraphs, the résumé should look something like this.

finish formatting

The résumé needs a bit more formatting before it's complete. Here are some suggestions.

Select each company name and use the Bold button on the Formatting toolbar (Windows) or Formatting Palette (Mac OS) to make it bold.

Select each school or training organization name and use the Bold button on the Formatting toolbar (Windows) or Formatting Palette (Mac OS) to make it bold.

Select each job title and use the Italic button on the Formatting toolbar (Windows) or Formatting Palette (Mac OS) to make it italic.

Here's what your résumé might look like when you've finished applying formatting.

MARIA LANGER
12345 Main Street, Suite A
Wickenburg, AZ 85390
v: 928/684-1111   f: 928/684-2222
maria@theflyingm.com

OBJECTIVE
To obtain work as a helicopter tour/charter pilot and/or Robinson helicopter ferry pilot.

QUALIFICATIONS
- Over 1,000 helicopter hours as pilot in command
- Extensive flight time in Robinson R22, Robinson R44, and Bell 206L1 helicopters
- Numerous cross-country flights in excess of 300 miles
- All Robinson Helicopter Company requirements for ferrying R22 and R44 helicopters in the southwestern United States.

EMPLOYMENT HISTORY

Papillon Airways, Grand Canyon, AZ   April 2004 to Present
Pilot/Captain
  I fly Bell 206L1-C30P helicopters on tours of Grand Canyon in a variety of challenging conditions. As Captain, I have direct responsibility for the operation of my assigned aircraft and the safety of my passengers.

Flying M Air, LLC, Wickenburg, AZ   October 2001 to Present
Owner/Pilot
  I fly Robinson R22 and Robinson R44 helicopters on part 91 tours of the Wickenburg area. As owner/operator of the company, I am responsible for all aspects of the business, including finances, maintenance arrangements, regulation compliance, and day-to-day operations.

Flying M Productions, Wickenburg, AZ   May 1990 to Present
Freelance Writer
  I am the author of over 50 technical books and over 100 articles for computer magazines. I have also written about helicopters and aviation for Sport Aviation, SW Aviator, and America's Flyways.

Automatic Data Processing, Roseland, NJ   August 1987 to May 1990
Senior Financial Analyst
  Worked on special projects to help management analyze business performance and trends. Created automated analysis applications with Lotus 1-2-3.

New York City Comptroller's Office, New York, NY   July 1982 to August 1987
Field Audit Supervisor
  Worked my way up from starting position as an auditor to supervisor in less than two years. Supervised a staff of 13 auditors working throughout New York City.

EDUCATION

Papillon Airways, Grand Canyon, AZ   April 2004
Turbine Transition Training for Bell 206L1-C30P

Robinson Helicopter Company, Torrance, CA   October 2002
Factory Safety Course

Hofstra University, Hempstead, NY   September 1978 to May 1982
BBA with Highest Honors in Accounting

justify page

If your résumé is brief, it may look like it's all bunched up at the top of the paper when printed. You can fix this with the page justification feature.

1 In Windows, choose Page Setup from the File menu to display the Page Setup dialog…

…or in Mac OS, choose Document from the Format menu to display the Document dialog.

justify page (cont'd)

2 Click the Layout tab (Windows) or button (Mac OS).

Page Setup dialog (Windows):

Margins | Paper | **Layout**

Section
Section start: New page
☐ Suppress endnotes

Headers and footers
☐ Different odd and even
☐ Different first page
From edge: Header: 0.5"
Footer: 0.5"

Page
Vertical alignment: Justified

Preview
Apply to:
Whole document

Line Numbers... | Borders...
Default... | OK | Cancel

Document dialog (Mac OS):

Margins | **Layout**

Section start: New page

Headers and Footers
☐ Different odd and even
☐ Different first page

Vertical alignment: Justified
☐ Suppress endnotes

Line Numbers...
Borders...

Preview

Apply to: Whole document

Default... | Page Setup... | Cancel | OK

3 Choose Justified from the Vertical alignment drop-down list (Windows) or pop-up menu (Mac OS).

4 Click OK.

The page contents are distributed vertically between the top and bottom margins.

MARIA LANGER
12345 Main Street, Suite A
Wickenburg, AZ 85390
v: 928/684-1111 f: 928/684-2222
maria@theflyingm.com

OBJECTIVE
To obtain work as a helicopter tour/charter pilot and/or Robinson helicopter ferry pilot

QUALIFICATIONS
- Over 1,000 helicopter hours as pilot in command
- Extensive flight time in Robinson R22, Robinson R44, and Bell 206L1 helicopters
- Numerous cross-country flights in excess of 300 miles

EMPLOYMENT HISTORY
Papillon Airways, Grand Canyon, AZ   April 2004 to Present
Pilot/Captain
  I fly Bell 206L1-C30P helicopters on tours of Grand Canyon in a variety of challenging conditions. As Captain, I have direct responsibility for the operation of my assigned aircraft and the safety of my passengers.

Flying M Air, LLC, Wickenburg, AZ   October 2001 to Present
Owner/Pilot
  I fly Robinson R22 and Robinson R44 helicopters on part 91 tours of the Wickenburg area. As owner/operator of the company, I am responsible for all aspects of the business, including finances, maintenance arrangements, regulation compliance, and day-to-day operations.

Flying M Productions, Wickenburg, AZ   May 1990 to Present
Freelance Writer
  I am the author of over 50 technical books and over 100 articles for computer magazines. I have also written about helicopters and aviation for Sport Aviation, SW Aviator, and America's Flyways.

EDUCATION
Papillon Airways, Grand Canyon, AZ   April 2004
Turbine Transition Training for Bell 206L1-C30P

Hofstra University, Hempstead, NY   September 1978 to May 1982
BBA with Highest Honors in Accounting

prepare a résumé

insert a page break

If your résumé is very long, it might require two pages to print. Although it's best to limit your résumé to one page, if you can't edit it to make it shorter, you might find it necessary to insert a manual page break to prevent the page break from occurring in the middle of a paragraph or some other undesired location.

1 Position the insertion point at the beginning of the line you want to appear at the top of the second page.

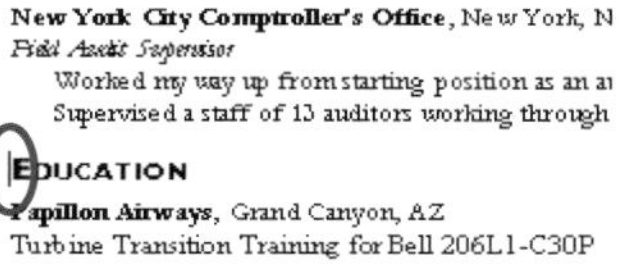

New York City Comptroller's Office, New York, N
Field Audit Supervisor
   Worked my way up from starting position as an a
   Supervised a staff of 13 auditors working through

EDUCATION
Papillon Airways, Grand Canyon, AZ
Turbine Transition Training for Bell 206L1-C30P

In Windows:

2 Choose Break from the Insert menu to display the Break dialog.

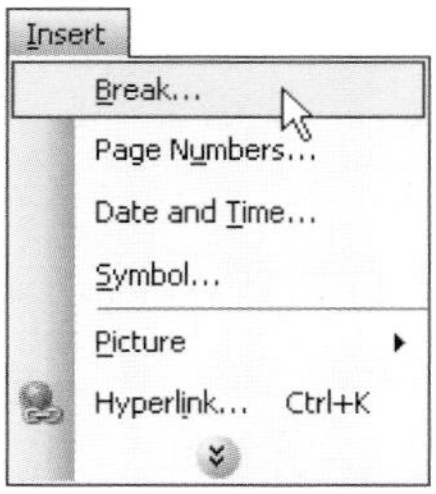

[Insert menu shown: Break..., Page Numbers..., Date and Time..., Symbol..., Picture, Hyperlink... Ctrl+K]

3 Select Page break.

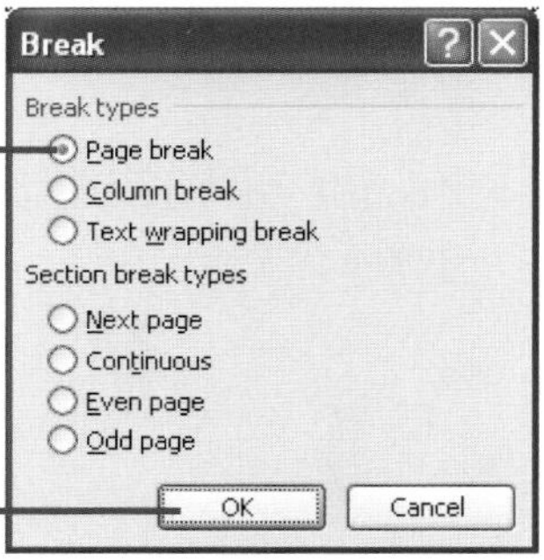

[Break dialog: Break types — Page break, Column break, Text wrapping break; Section break types — Next page, Continuous, Even page, Odd page; OK, Cancel]

4 Click OK.

In Mac OS:

2 Choose Page Break from the Break submenu under the Insert menu.

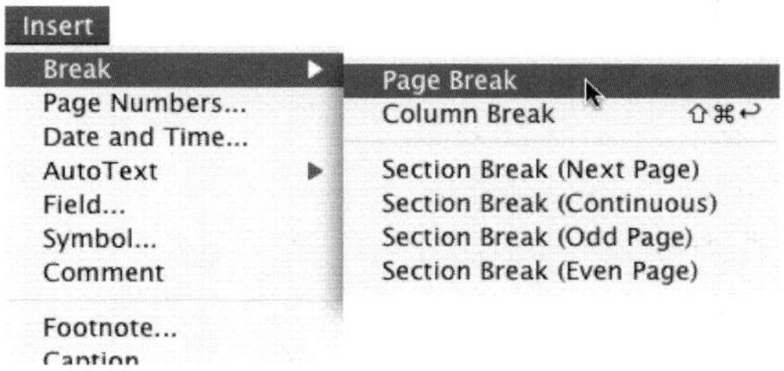

[Insert menu shown: Break ▶ (Page Break, Column Break ⇧⌘↵, Section Break (Next Page), Section Break (Continuous), Section Break (Odd Page), Section Break (Even Page)); Page Numbers..., Date and Time..., AutoText ▶, Field..., Symbol..., Comment, Footnote..., Caption]

A page break is inserted in the document at the insertion point. The text after it is forced to the next page.

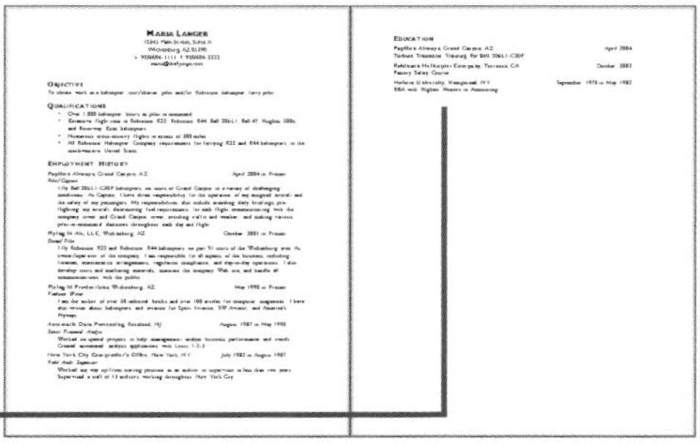

finish up

Once you're satisfied with your résumé, it's time to finish up. For more information about any of these steps, consult Chapter 2.

1 Save the résumé. When you use the Save command, Word displays the Save As dialog. Be sure to save the document in your My Documents (Windows) or Documents (Mac OS) folder or some other location where you can easily find it.

2 Print the résumé. Use the Print command to print out a copy. Use good quality paper and make sure your printer has a good toner or ink jet cartridge so print quality is good.

3 Close the document file. If you're done working with the résumé, close it.

extra bits

enter qualifications p. 68

- When entering qualifications, don't get carried away. Limit yourself to 4 or 5 items.

- Use parallel constructions when composing list items. For example, if the first item on the list is a full sentence, all items on the list should be a full sentence. If the first item on the list is first person past tense, all items on the list should be first person past tense. Consult a style guide such as "The Elements of Style" for help.

format headings pp. 71-72

- To copy font formatting using the Format Painter, you must select the text with the formatting you want to copy before clicking or double-clicking the Format Painter button.

- Double-clicking the Format Painter button turns it on for multiple uses. If you only wanted to copy a format to one destination, click the Format Painter button once and select the destination text. The cursor returns to normal after one use.

format items pp. 73-74

- To copy paragraph formatting using the Format Painter, you can click anywhere in the paragraph with the formatting you want to copy before clicking or double-clicking the Format Painter button. Selecting the entire paragraph is not required.

- If the dates of employment do not shift to the right as shown on page 74 after setting up the tab stop or using the Format Painter, it's probably because you didn't press the Tab key immediately before the date. Position the insertion point to the left of the date and press the Tab key. The text should shift.

extra bits

indent descriptions p. 75

- If the ruler is not showing, choose Ruler from the View menu to display it.

justify page pp. 77-78

- If your résumé is very short, adjust your margins so they're at least 1.5 inches at the top and bottom. Otherwise, you might wind up with big gaps between lines of text. For more on how to set margins, see Chapter 3.

insert a page break p. 79

- You can only insert a manual page break before an automatic one. Inserting a manual page break after an automatic page break will break the document into more pages.

- To delete a page break, position the insertion point right at the beginning of the page and press Backspace (Windows) or Delete (Mac OS).

prepare a résumé

6. create
business cards

Business cards are an important part of anyone's personal marketing toolkit. Not only do they provide a handy way to distribute your contact information to acquaintances and business associates, but they help reinforce your company's business identity.

Word's label feature makes it easy to create business cards on special business card stock. This paper, manufactured by companies such as Avery, enables you to print 10 standard-sized business cards on a single sheet. When the page emerges from your printer, simply tear the cards apart at the perforations.

This chapter explains how to create business cards that include complete contact information and a company logo.

open the labels dialog

You use the Labels tab of the Envelopes and Labels dialog (Windows) or the Labels dialog (Mac OS) to create a business card document.

In Windows:

1 Choose Envelopes and Labels from the Letters and Mailings submenu under the Tools menu.

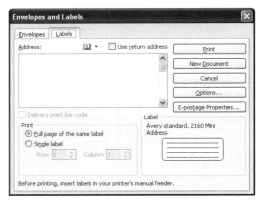

2 In the Envelopes and Labels dialog that appears, click the Labels tab to display its options.

In Mac OS:

Choose Labels from the Tools menu.

The Labels dialog appears.

select card product

The first task is to select the type of paper you will be using for your business cards. In this example, I'm using Avery product number 5371.

1 Click the Options button in the Labels tab of the Envelopes and Labels dialog (Windows) or the Labels dialog (Mac OS).

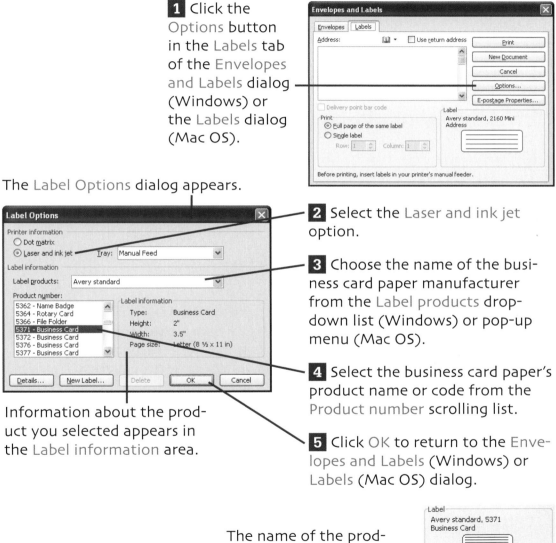

The Label Options dialog appears.

Information about the product you selected appears in the Label information area.

2 Select the Laser and ink jet option.

3 Choose the name of the business card paper manufacturer from the Label products drop-down list (Windows) or pop-up menu (Mac OS).

4 Select the business card paper's product name or code from the Product number scrolling list.

5 Click OK to return to the Envelopes and Labels (Windows) or Labels (Mac OS) dialog.

The name of the product you selected should appear in the Label area.

create business cards

enter card text

Now, enter the text you want to appear on every card.

1 Position the blinking insertion point in the Address box of the Labels tab of the Envelopes and Labels dialog (Windows) or Labels dialog (Mac OS).

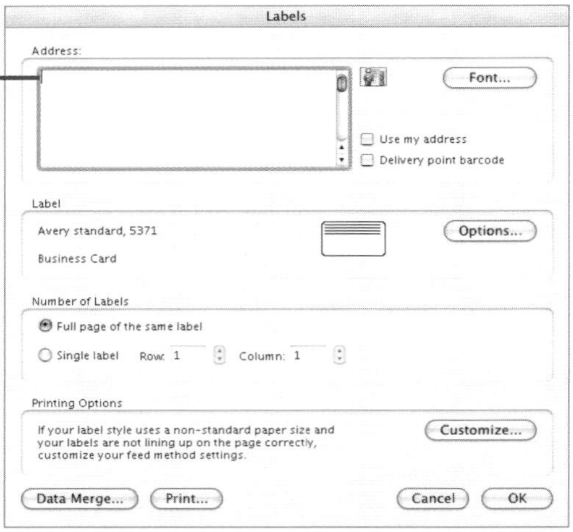

2 Type in all the contact information you want to appear on the card. Press Enter (Windows) or Return (Mac OS) at the end of each line.

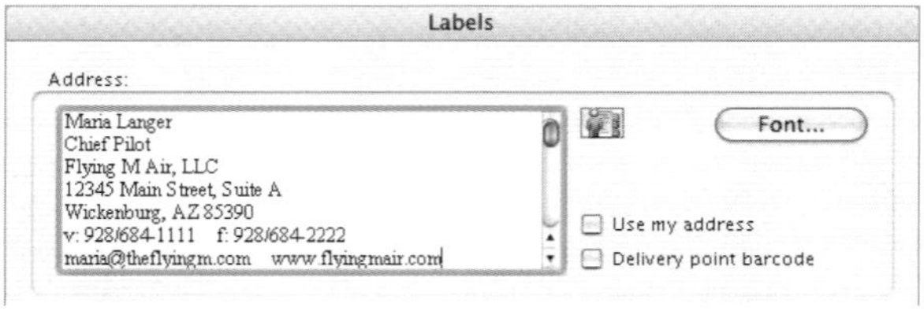

As shown here, I included my name, title, company name, address, phone numbers, e-mail address, and Web site.

create business cards

create the document

When you save your settings in the Envelopes and Labels dialog (Windows) or Labels dialog (Mac OS), Word creates the business card document.

In Windows, click the New Document button in the Labels tab of the Envelopes and Labels dialog.

In Mac OS, click the OK button in the Labels dialog.

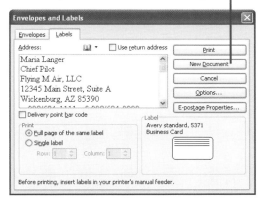

Word creates a new document that uses its table feature to lay out the ten business cards.

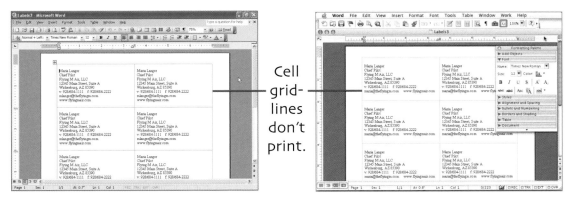

Cell gridlines don't print.

Windows

Mac OS

format the text

You may want to format the business card text with a different font, size, and style. Just apply formatting to one card; you'll be copying that card to replace the other cards before printing.

Maria Langer
Chief Pilot
Flying M Air, LLC
12345 Main Street, Suite A
Wickenburg, AZ 85390
v: 928/684-1111   f: 928/684-2222
mlanger@theflyingm.com
www.flyingmair.com

1 Select the text you want to format in the first (top-left) business card on the page.

2 Choose Font from the Format menu to display the Font dialog.

3 Set font formatting options as desired. If you need help, refer to Chapter 2.

4 Click OK to save your settings.

5 Repeat steps 1–4 for all the text you want to format in the first card.

Here's what my card looks like so far. I applied 11 pt bold Papyrus font to my name, 12 pt Gill Sans font to my company name, and 10 pt Gill Sans font to the remaining text.

Maria Langer
Chief Pilot
Flying M Air, LLC
12345 Main Street, Suite A
Wickenburg, AZ 85390
v: 928/684-1111   f: 928/684-2222
mlanger@theflyingm.com   www.flyingmair.com

88   **create business cards**

6 Select all the text on the first card.

7 Click the Center button on the Formatting toolbar (Windows) or the Align Center button in the Alignment and Spacing area of the Formatting Palette (Mac OS).

The text is centered.

insert an image

Inserting a small image or logo helps reinforce your company identity.

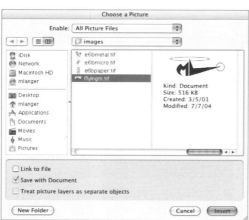

1 Position the insertion point to the left of the first letter in the first card.

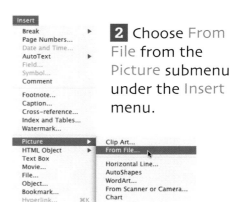

2 Choose From File from the Picture submenu under the Insert menu.

3 Use the Insert Picture (Windows) or Choose a Picture (Mac OS) dialog that appears to locate and select the image you want to insert. If you need help using this dialog, consult Chapter 2.

4 Click Insert.

The image is inserted in the first card.

5 Press Enter (Windows) or Return (Mac OS) to place the image in its own paragraph.

6 If necessary, follow the instructions on page 49 to resize the image.

When you're done, the first card might look something like this.

create business cards

duplicate the card

When the first card on the page looks the way you want it to, duplicate it to replace the other cards, which are acting as placeholders, on the page.

1 Position the mouse pointer near the bottom-right corner of the first card.

2 Triple-click the mouse button. The entire card becomes selected.

3 Choose Copy from the Edit menu. The first card is copied to the clipboard.

4 Press the Tab key to select the next card.

5 Choose Paste Cells from the Edit menu.

The selected card is replaced with a copy of the first card.

6 Repeat steps 4 and 5 to replace the remaining cards with the finished card.

When you're finished, the document should look like the one on the next page.

finish your cards

When the document is complete, you can save, print, and close it.

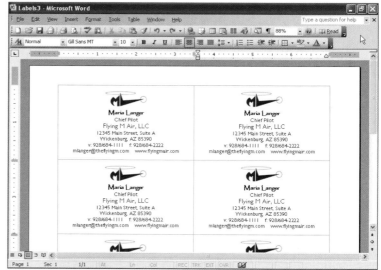

1 Save the business cards. Be sure to save the business card document in your My Documents (Windows) or Documents (Mac OS) folder or some other location where you can easily find it.

2 Print the business cards. Insert the business card paper into your printer's print tray or manual feeder and use the Print command to print a sheet of business cards. You can then tear along the perforations to separate the sheet of cards into ten individual cards.

3 Close the document file. If you're done working with the business cards, close the document.

create business cards

extra bits

open the labels dialog p. 84

- You must have at least one document open to use the Envelopes and Labels (Windows) or Labels (Mac OS) command. If no documents are open, click the New Blank Document button on the standard toolbar to create one. You can then choose the Labels command.

select card product p. 85

- You can get the name of the business card paper manufacturer and the product number from the package the business card paper comes in.

enter card text p. 86

- The Use return address (Windows) or Use my address (Mac OS) check box must be turned off to enter custom text in the Address box in the Labels tab of the Envelopes and Labels dialog (Windows) or Labels dialog (Mac OS).

- For best results, don't enter more than 7 or 8 lines of text in your business card. If you enter more, you won't be able to fit a logo or other graphic.

- The Mac OS version of Word enables you to format business card (or label) text right inside the Labels dialog. Just click the Font button to display the Font dialog and format selected text in the Address box.

create the document p. 87

- If the gray table gridlines do not appear, choose Show Gridlines from the Table menu.

duplicate the card p. 91

- Do not press the Tab key after pasting in the last card on the page. Doing so will create a new row in the table and mess up the document. If you do this by mistake (oops!), choose Undo Next Cell from the Edit menu.

7. produce a flyer

Flyers are a great way to spread the word about a product or event. Not only can they summarize all the important information you need to share, but they're easy to create and inexpensive to reproduce in quantity.

In this chapter, we'll produce a flyer like the one shown here to advertise a special, limited-time offer. The flyer will include page borders, formatted text, and a positioned graphic. As you work through this project, you'll learn plenty of techniques to help you create your own flyers and single-page brochures.

prepare a document

Start by creating a new document and changing the view.

1 Click the New Blank Document button on the Standard toolbar to create a new document.

2 Click the Print Layout View button (Windows) or Page Layout View button (Mac OS) at the bottom of the document window. This switches you to a layout view where you can see the document the way it will print.

3 Choose Whole Page from the Zoom drop-down list on the Standard toolbar.

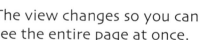

The view changes so you can see the entire page at once.

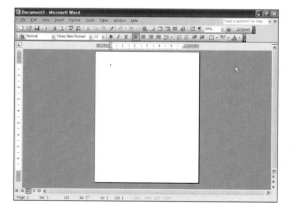

produce a flyer

set page options

Next, set the margins and other page layout options.

1 In Windows, choose Page Setup from the File menu...

...or in Mac OS, choose Document from the Format menu.

2 In the Page Setup (Windows) or Document (Mac OS) dialog that appears, click the Margins tab (Windows) or button (Mac OS).

3 Type .75 in the Top, Bottom, Left, and Right boxes.

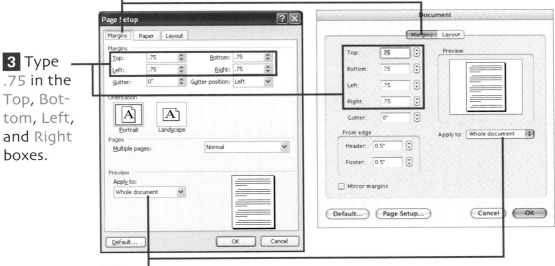

4 Choose Whole document from the Apply to drop-down list (Windows) or pop-up menu (Mac OS).

set page options (cont'd)

5 Click the Layout tab (Windows) or button (Mac OS) to display layout options.

6 Choose Center from the Vertical alignment drop-down list (Windows) or pop-up menu (Mac OS).

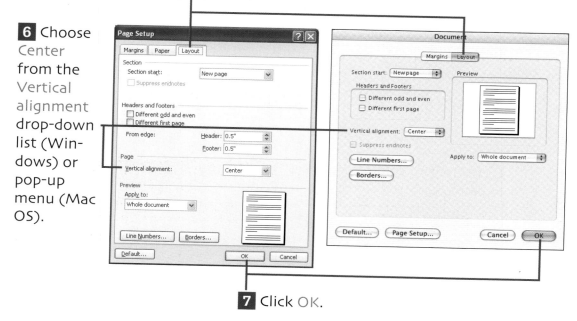

7 Click OK.

produce a flyer

set default formats

Because the text on this flyer will be large and we're working with it in a reduced view, we'll set a default font and font size now. We'll also add some spacing before each paragraph to separate the paragraphs a bit. This will make the text easy to read while we work and give us an idea of how much text will fit on the page.

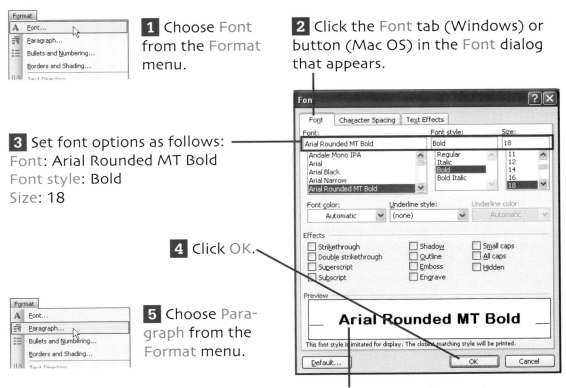

1 Choose Font from the Format menu.

2 Click the Font tab (Windows) or button (Mac OS) in the Font dialog that appears.

3 Set font options as follows:
Font: Arial Rounded MT Bold
Font style: Bold
Size: 18

4 Click OK.

5 Choose Para-graph from the Format menu.

The Preview area shows what your settings will look like when applied to text.

set default formats (cont'd)

6 Click the Indents and Spacing tab (Windows) or button (Mac OS).

7 Choose Left from the Alignment drop-down list (Windows) or pop-up menu (Mac OS).

8 Type 24 pt in the Before box in the Spacing area.

9 Click OK.

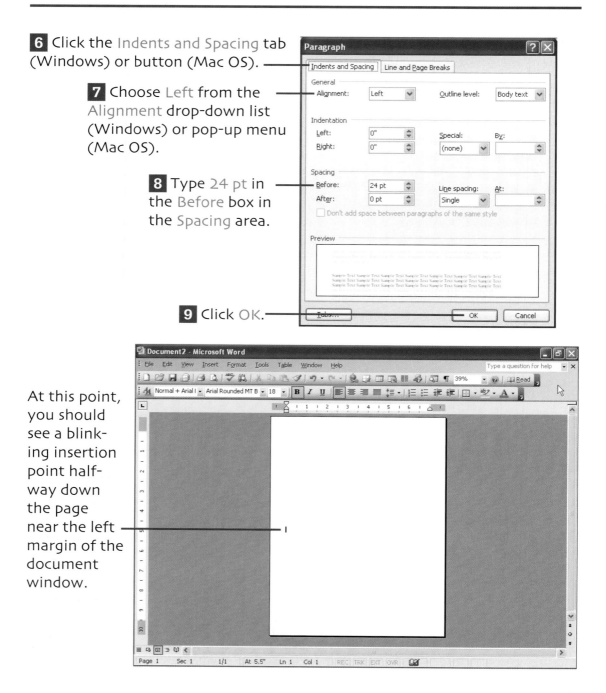

At this point, you should see a blinking insertion point halfway down the page near the left margin of the document window.

produce a flyer

add a page border

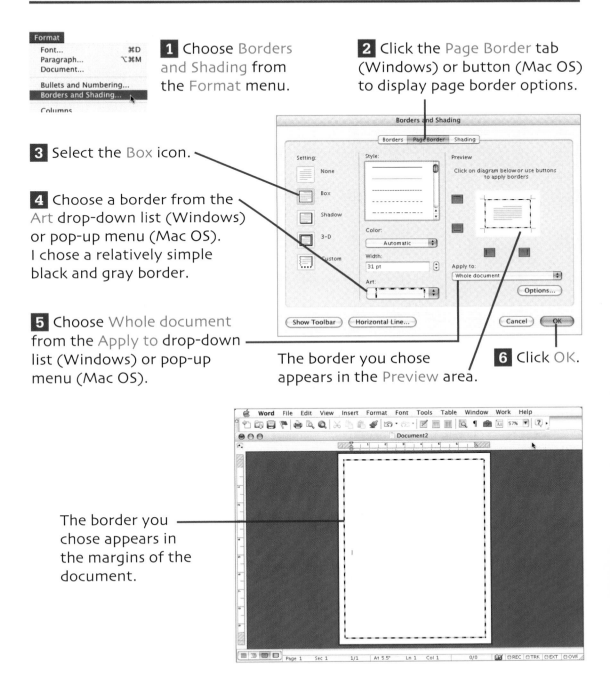

1 Choose Borders and Shading from the Format menu.

2 Click the Page Border tab (Windows) or button (Mac OS) to display page border options.

3 Select the Box icon.

4 Choose a border from the Art drop-down list (Windows) or pop-up menu (Mac OS). I chose a relatively simple black and gray border.

5 Choose Whole document from the Apply to drop-down list (Windows) or pop-up menu (Mac OS).

The border you chose appears in the Preview area.

6 Click OK.

The border you chose appears in the margins of the document.

enter text

The next step is to enter the text you want to appear on the flyer.

Type the text in, using text entry techniques discussed in Chapter 2.

When you're finished, it might
look something like this.

```
Special Offer
this August only

Sunrise Helicopter Tours

See the desert come to life in the early morning
light.

Enjoy cool air and a smooth, turbulence-free
flight.

Flights depart at 5:30 AM
30 minutes: $79/person
60 minutes: $159/person

Call for Reservations:
Flying M Air
684-1111|
```

When you press Enter (Windows) or Return (Mac OS), Word starts a new paragraph with 24 points of spacing above it.

If you want to start a new line without the additional spacing above it, press Shift-Enter (Windows) or Shift-Return (Mac OS). This inserts a line break, thus creating a new line in the same paragraph.

produce a flyer

format text

Once you have all the text you want on the flyer and can see how it fits, you can go back and format specific text to make it larger or smaller. You can also change fonts, styles, and colors. You do all this with the Font dialog.

1 Select the text you want to reformat.

2 Choose Font from the Format menu.

3 Click the Font tab (Windows) or button (Mac OS) in the Font dialog that appears.

4 Set options in the Font dialog to change the appearance of selected text.

The Preview area shows you what the text will look like.

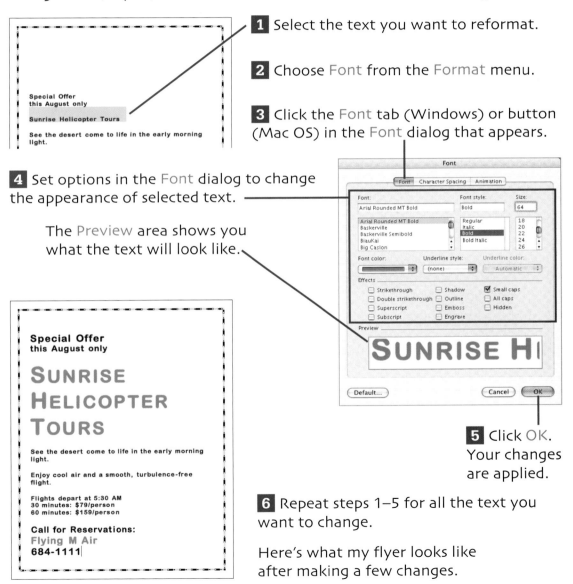

5 Click OK. Your changes are applied.

6 Repeat steps 1–5 for all the text you want to change.

Here's what my flyer looks like after making a few changes.

add a bulleted list

If your flyer includes a list of items, you can format them with bullets so they're easily recognized as a list.

1 Select the paragraphs that you want to format as a list.

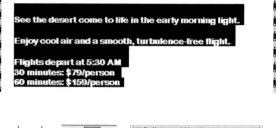

2 Click the Bullets button on the Standard toolbar (Windows) or the Bullets button in the Bullets and Numbering area of the Formatting Palette (Mac OS).

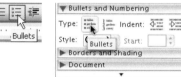

The paragraphs you selected are formatted as a bulleted list.

position an image

You can include an image in your flyer and position it exactly where you want it to appear.

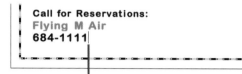

1 Position the insertion point at the end of the document.

2 Follow the instructions on pages 47–48 to insert an image file into the document.

3 If your image needs to be resized, follow the instructions on page 49 to resize it.

At this point, your document might look like this. As you can see, inserting the image caused a second page to be added to my document. I'll fix that when I move the image.

4 Double-click the image to display the Format Picture dialog.

5 Click the Layout tab (Windows) or button (Mac OS).

6 Select the Square icon under Wrapping style.

7 Click OK.

position an image (cont'd)

The image shifts and circles (Windows) or boxes (Mac OS) appear at its corners and sides.

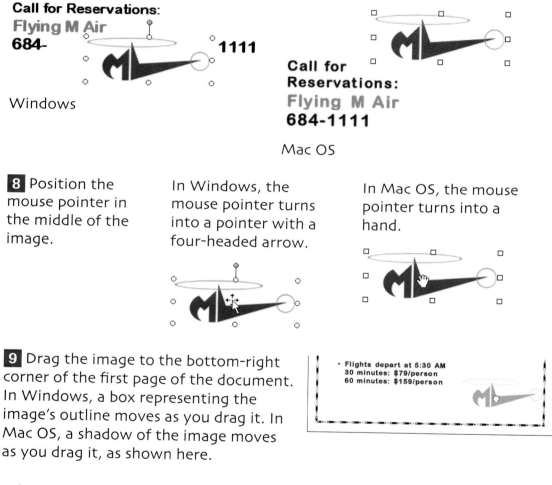

Windows

Mac OS

8 Position the mouse pointer in the middle of the image.

In Windows, the mouse pointer turns into a pointer with a four-headed arrow.

In Mac OS, the mouse pointer turns into a hand.

9 Drag the image to the bottom-right corner of the first page of the document. In Windows, a box representing the image's outline moves as you drag it. In Mac OS, a shadow of the image moves as you drag it, as shown here.

When you release the mouse button, the image appears in its new position. Any text that would be hidden shifts so it wraps around the image.

produce a flyer

print in color (Windows)

If you have a color printer and have included color in your flyer, you should print it in color.

1 Choose Print from the File menu to display the Print dialog.

2 Choose your color printer from the Name drop-down list.

3 Click the Properties button to display the Properties dialog for your printer.

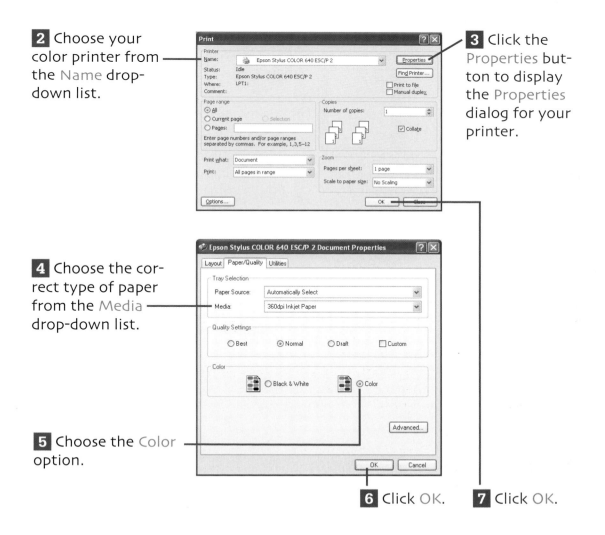

4 Choose the correct type of paper from the Media drop-down list.

5 Choose the Color option.

6 Click OK.

7 Click OK.

print in color (Mac OS)

If you have a color printer and have included color in your flyer, you should print it in color.

1 Choose Print from the File menu to display the Print dialog.

2 Choose your color printer from the Printer pop-up menu.

3 Choose Print Settings from the third pop-up menu to display settings for your printer.

4 Choose the correct type of paper from the Media Type pop-up menu.

5 Choose Color from the Ink pop-up menu.

6 Click Print.

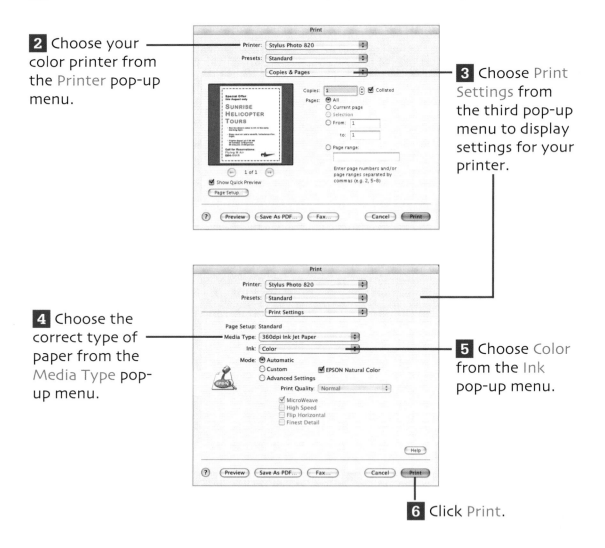

produce a flyer

finish your flyer

When you're finished creating and printing your flyer, you can save and close it.

1 Save the flyer. Be sure to save the document in your My Documents (Windows) or Documents (Mac OS) folder or some other location where you can easily find it.

2 Close the document file. If you're done working with the flyer, close the document.

extra bits

set page options pp. 97-98

- Some printers do not allow small margins. If you set margins smaller than that allowed by your printer, a dialog like the one shown here will appear. Click Fix to tell Microsoft Word to adjust the margins to the smallest allowed measurement.

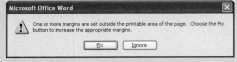

add a page border p. 101

- The first time you use the Art drop-down list in Word for Windows, a dialog may appear, telling you that the feature is not installed. Click the Yes button in that dialog and follow the instructions that appear onscreen to install border art.

enter text p. 102
format text p. 103
add a bulleted list p. 104

- The trick to entering and formatting text on a flyer is to make sure all the text appears on a single page. If your text stretches to two pages, you can get it back down to one page by editing out unnecessary text or making font sizes smaller.

position an image pp. 105-106

- When you set the Wrapping style option to Square in the Layout screen of the Format Picture dialog, you place the image on its own graphic layer so it can be moved anywhere on a page.

print in color pp. 107-108

- The Properties dialog (Windows) and Print dialog (Mac OS) may offer different options than those illustrated on pages 107 and 108. If you're not sure how to set these options to print in color, check the documentation that came with your printer.

110   produce a flyer

8. print an envelope

Microsoft Word has a built-in envelope-printing feature that makes it easy to create professional-looking envelopes for all of your correspondence.

As you'll see in this chapter, Word can automatically address an envelope based on text in a letter or other document. Or you can create an envelope on-the-fly with any address you want to use.

Maria Langer
Flying M Air, LLC
12345 Main Street, Suite A
Wickenburg, AZ 85390

‖₁‖₁₁₁‖₁₁‖₁₁₁‖₁₁₁₁‖₁₁₁‖
John Smith
Amenities Director
The GreenWater Resort & Casino
12345 Resort Drive
Quartzite, AZ 85344

select an addressee

If you want to print an envelope for a person you've already written a letter to, Word can address the envelope based on the address already typed in the letter. (If you prefer to create an envelope on-the-fly, you can skip this step.)

1 Open the letter to the person you want to print an envelope for. (See Chapter 2 for more information about opening existing Word documents.)

2 Select the address in the document.

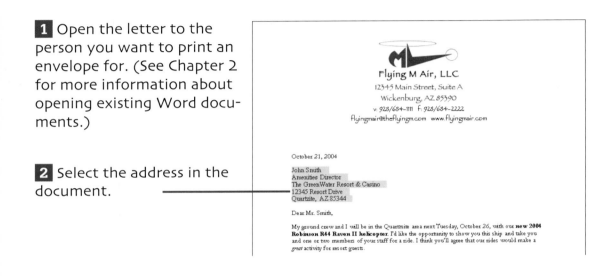

open the envelope dialog

You create an envelope with the Envelopes tab of the Envelopes and Labels dialog (Windows) or with the Envelope dialog (Mac OS). (For simplicity's sake, I'll refer to this as simply the Envelope dialog when discussing the Windows and Mac OS versions of this dialog at the same time.)

In Windows:

1 Choose Envelopes and Labels from the Letters and Mailings submenu under the Tools menu to display the Envelopes and Labels dialog.

In Mac OS:

Choose Envelopes from the Tools menu.

The Envelope dialog appears.

2 Click the Envelopes tab to display envelope options.

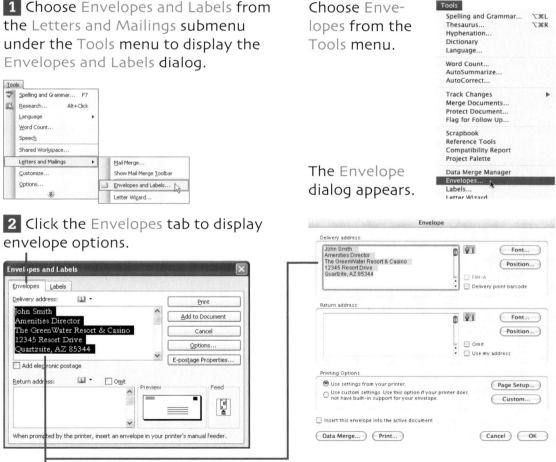

As you can see here, if you selected an addressee before opening the Envelope dialog, the Delivery address box in the dialog is already filled in.

enter addresses

The Envelope dialog has two boxes for envelope addresses: Delivery address and Return address.

1 If the Delivery address box is not already filled in correctly, click in the Delivery address box and type the name and address of the person you want to address the envelope to. Be sure to press Enter (Windows) or Return (Mac OS) after each line.

Jane Jones
1313 Mockingbird Lane
Munster, AL 54236

2 To include a return address on the envelope, click in the Return address box and type in your name and address. Be sure to press Enter (Windows) or Return (Mac OS) after each line.

Maria Langer
Flying M Air, LLC
12345 Main Street, Suite A
Wickenburg, AZ 85390

To omit the return address from the envelope—perhaps you're printing an envelope that already has a return address printed on it—turn on the Omit check box.

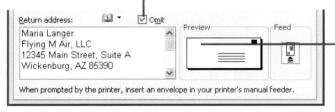

Return address: ☑ Omit

Maria Langer
Flying M Air, LLC
12345 Main Street, Suite A
Wickenburg, AZ 85390

Preview   Feed

When prompted by the printer, insert an envelope in your printer's manual feeder.

In Windows, when you turn on the Omit check box, the Preview area of the Envelopes tab of the Envelopes and Labels dialog changes to show that a return address will not print on the envelope.

set address fonts (Windows)

You can customize the appearance of an envelope by setting font options for the delivery and return addresses.

1 Click the Options button in the Envelopes tab of the Envelopes and Labels dialog.

2 Click the Envelope Options tab in the Envelope Options dialog that appears.

3 Click the Font button in the area for the address you want to format.

A font dialog for the type of address you are formatting appears.

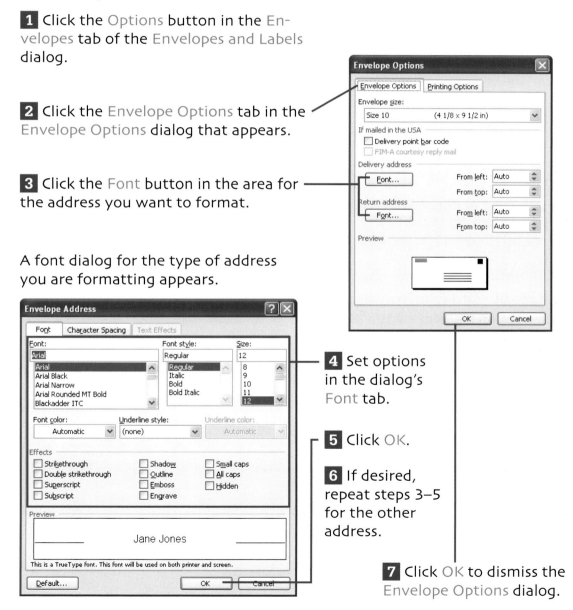

4 Set options in the dialog's Font tab.

5 Click OK.

6 If desired, repeat steps 3–5 for the other address.

7 Click OK to dismiss the Envelope Options dialog.

print an envelope

set address fonts (Mac OS)

You can customize the appearance of an envelope by setting font options for the delivery and return addresses.

1 In the Envelope dialog, click the Font button in the area for the address you want to format.

A Font dialog appears.

2 Set options in the dialog's Font tab.

3 Click OK.

The appearance of the text for the address you formatted changes to show your new settings.

4 If desired, repeat steps 1–3 for the other address.

print an envelope

include a bar code

You can include a delivery point bar code—also known as a POSTNET bar code—for the delivery address. This special code is used by the post office's routing equipment to read the zip code and speed your letter on its way.

In Windows:

1 Click the Options button in the Envelopes tab of the Envelopes and Labels dialog.

2 Click the Envelope Options tab in the Envelope Options dialog that appears.

3 Turn on the Delivery point bar code check box. ──────

The Preview area changes to show a bar code above the delivery address. ──────

4 Click OK. ──────

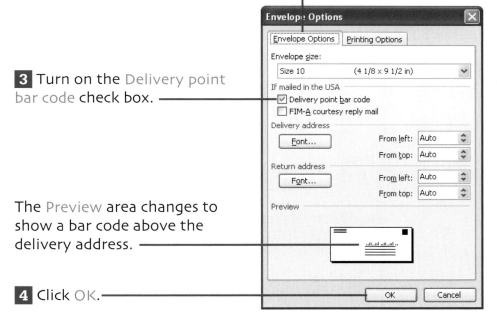

In Mac OS:

In the Envelope dialog, turn on the Delivery point barcode check box.

set printing options (Windows)

To ensure that your printer prints the envelope correctly the first time, set the envelope size and feed method.

1 Click the Feed button in the Envelopes tab of the Envelopes and Labels dialog.

When prompted by the printer, insert an envelope in your printer's manual feeder.

2 Set options in the Feed method area to specify how envelopes are fed into your printer.

Changing the Face up/Face down and Clockwise rotation settings changes the illustrations on the icons, like this:

The Printing Options tab of the Envelope Options dialog appears.

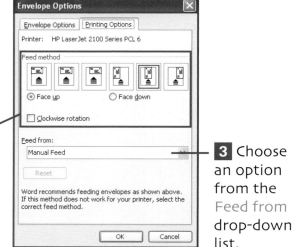

3 Choose an option from the Feed from drop-down list.

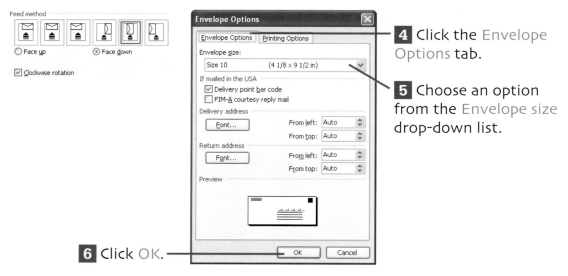

4 Click the Envelope Options tab.

5 Choose an option from the Envelope size drop-down list.

6 Click OK.

print an envelope

set printing options (Mac OS)

To ensure that your printer prints the envelope correctly the first time, set the envelope size and feed method.

1 Click the Custom button in the Envelope dialog.

The Custom Page Options dialog appears.

2 Choose an option from the Envelope size pop-up menu.

3 Set options in the Feed method area to specify how envelopes are fed into your printer.

Changing the Face up/Face down and Clockwise rotation settings changes the illustrations on the icons, like this:

4 Click OK.

print the envelope

When you're finished setting options in the Envelope dialog, you can print the envelope.

1 Put an envelope in the appropriate feed tray of your printer.

In Windows:

2 Click the Print button in the Envelopes tab of the Envelopes and Labels dialog.

The envelope prints immediately, without displaying a dialog.

In Mac OS:

2 Click the Print button in the Envelope dialog.

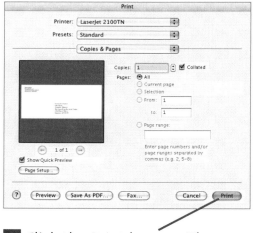

Word creates an envelope document and displays the Print dialog.

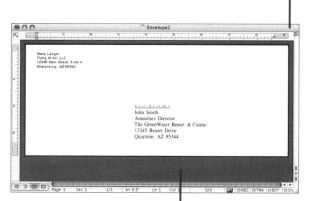

3 Click the Print button. The envelope prints.

4 Close the envelope document Word created. You don't have to save it.

print an envelope

extra bits

select an addressee p. 112

- Word is smart. In many cases, it can "guess" which text in a letter document is the address to use for an envelope's delivery address. Try it for yourself! Skip step 2 on page 112 and see what happens when you open the Envelope dialog.

enter addresses p. 114

- If you use Outlook (Windows) or Entourage (Mac OS) to maintain a contacts database, you can click the Address Book button near the Delivery address or Return address box to choose a contact to insert.

- In Word for Macintosh, you can turn on the Use my address check box to insert your name and address in the Return address box.

- You must turn on the Omit check box if you don't want to include a return address on an envelope. If you fail to do so, Word may print placeholder text in the return address area of the envelope when it prints.

- In Windows, if you enter a new return address (one that wasn't already in the Return address box), when you finish printing the envelope Windows will display a dialog asking if you want to save the return address as the default return address. Click Yes if you want that return address to automatically be entered each time you create an envelope.

include a bar code p. 117

- To include a bar code on an envelope, the delivery address must include a zip code.

- Bar codes can only be created for U.S. addresses.

- If you turn on the Delivery point bar code check box option for an envelope, you can also turn on the FIM-A check box. This option, which is designed for courtesy reply envelopes, prints a code that identifies the address side of the envelope.

extra bits

set printing options (Mac OS) p. 119

- If you're not sure how to set printing options, select the Use settings from your printer radio button in the Printing Options area of the Envelope dialog. In most cases, these settings are correct and the envelope will come out fine.

print the envelope p. 120

- In Windows, you can add the envelope to the currently active document as a new page in the document. You can then print the envelope when you print the document. Click the Add to Document button in the Envelopes tab of the Envelopes and Labels dialog.

- In Mac OS, you can save the envelope document Word created as part of the printing process. Just choose Save from the File menu and use the Save As dialog that appears to name and save the envelope. You can then open and print it again another time.

print an envelope

9. create return address labels

Return address labels make it quick and easy to finish off correspondence—whether you're mailing bills or sending out packages to customers. With Word's label feature, you can create professional-looking return address labels in minutes.

But take a moment to think about what return address labels really are. They're preprinted stickers that all say the same thing. If you take that idea a step further, it's easy to imagine using this feature to create stickers you can use to label products, spread your company slogan, or even clearly identify the owner of the books and videos you loan to friends.

This chapter explains how you can create a full page of identical labels that you can use for return addresses or anything else.

open the labels dialog

You use the Labels tab of the Envelopes and Labels dialog (Windows) or the Labels dialog (Mac OS) to create a label document.

In Windows:

1 Choose Envelopes and Labels from the Letters and Mailings submenu under the Tools menu.

2 In the Envelopes and Labels dialog that appears, click the Labels tab to display its options.

In Mac OS:

Choose Labels from the Tools menu.

The Labels dialog appears.

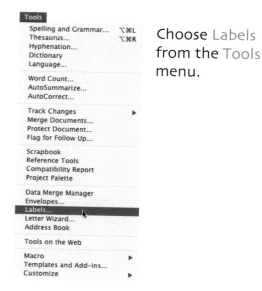

create return address labels

select label product

The first task is to select the type of labels you will be using.

1 Click the Options button in the Labels tab of the Envelopes and Labels dialog (Windows) or the Labels dialog (Mac OS).

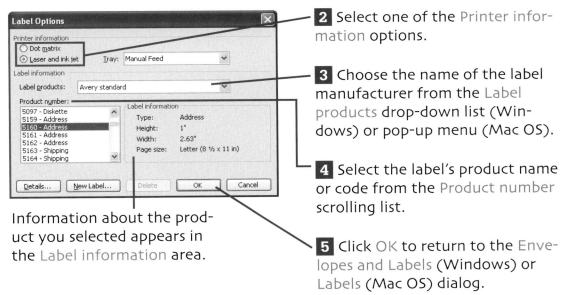

The Label Options dialog appears.

2 Select one of the Printer information options.

3 Choose the name of the label manufacturer from the Label products drop-down list (Windows) or pop-up menu (Mac OS).

4 Select the label's product name or code from the Product number scrolling list.

Information about the product you selected appears in the Label information area.

5 Click OK to return to the Envelopes and Labels (Windows) or Labels (Mac OS) dialog.

create a custom label

If the labels you're using are not listed in the Label Options dialog, you can create custom settings for a label product. To do this, you'll need a sample of the label sheet and an accurate ruler.

1 Click the Options button in the Labels tab of the Envelopes and Labels dialog (Windows) or the Labels dialog (Mac OS).

The Label Options dialog appears.

Label Options

Printer information
- ○ Dot matrix
- ◉ Laser and ink jet

Label products: Avery standard

Product number:	Label information	
5096 – Diskette	Type:	Address
5097 – Diskette		
5160 – Address		
5161 – Address	Height:	1"
5162 – Address		
5163 – Shipping	Width:	2.63"
5164 – Shipping		
5165 – Full Sheet	Page size:	Letter (8 1/2 x 11 in)
5167 – Return Address		

Details...   New Label...   Delete   Cancel   OK

2 Select Laser and inkjet in the Printer information area.

3 Click the New Label button.

The New Custom laser dialog appears.

New Custom laser

Preview

Side margins
Top margin — Horizontal pitch
Vertical pitch — Width — Height
Number down
Number across

Label name: CompuLabel 1510R

Top margin:	0.5"	Label height:	1"
Side margin:	0.5"	Label width:	1.5"
Vertical pitch:	1"	Number across:	5
Horizontal pitch:	1.5"	Number down:	10

Page size: Letter (8 1/2 x 11 in)

Cancel   OK

4 Enter a name for your custom label in the Label name box.

5 Choose a size option from the Page size drop-down list (Windows) or pop-up menu (Mac OS).

create return address labels

Top margin:	0.5"	Label height:	1"
Side margin:	0.5"	Label width:	1.5"
Vertical pitch:	1"	Number across:	5
Horizontal pitch:	1.5"	Number down:	10

6 Type values into each box in the dialog, as follows:

Top margin is the distance from the top edge of the label sheet to the first label on the sheet.

Side margin is the distance from the left edge of the label sheet to the first label.

Vertical pitch is the distance from the top edge of the first label on the sheet to the top edge of the second label on the sheet. (This may be different from label height!)

Horizontal pitch is the distance from the left edge of the first label on the sheet to the left edge of the label to its right. (This may be different from label width!)

Label height is the distance from the top edge of a label to the bottom edge of the same label.

Label width is the distance from the left edge of a label to the right edge of the same label.

Number across is the number of labels across the page.

Number down is the number of labels down the page.

7 Click OK to save your custom settings.

The label you created appears in the Product number list of the Label Options dialog. Make sure it's selected if you want to use it now.

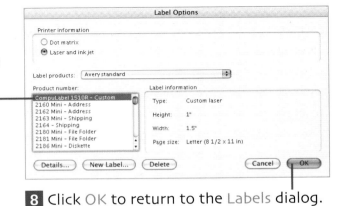

8 Click OK to return to the Labels dialog.

create return address labels

enter text

Now, enter the text you want to appear on every label.

1 Position the blinking insertion point in the Address box of the Labels tab of the Envelopes and Labels dialog (Windows) or Labels dialog (Mac OS).

Envelopes and Labels ☒

Envelopes | Labels

Address: 📖 ▾ ☐ Use return address

Print
New Document
Cancel
Options...
E-postage Properties...

☐ Delivery point bar code

Label
Avery standard, 5160
Address

Print
◉ Full page of the same label
○ Single label
Row: 1   Column: 1

Before printing, insert labels in your printer's manual feeder.

2 Type in all of the information you want to appear on the label. Press Enter (Windows) or Return (Mac OS) at the end of each line.

Envelopes and Labels ☒

Envelopes | Labels

Address: 📖 ▾ ☑ Use return address

Maria Langer
Flying M Air, LLC
12345 Main Street, Suite A
Wickenburg, AZ 85390

Print
New Document
Cancel
Options...
E-postage Properties...

☐ Delivery point bar code

Label
Avery standard, 5160
Address

Print
◉ Full page of the same label
○ Single label
Row: 1   Column: 1

Before printing, insert labels in your printer's manual feeder.

A quick way to enter your return address is to turn on the Use return address (Windows) or Use my address (Mac OS) check box.

3 Select the Full page of the same label option in the Print (Windows) or Number of Labels (Mac OS) area.

create return address labels

create the document

When you save your settings in the Envelopes and Labels dialog (Windows) or Labels dialog (Mac OS), Word creates the label document.

In Windows, click the New Document button in the Labels tab of the Envelopes and Labels dialog.

In Mac OS, click the OK button in the Labels dialog.

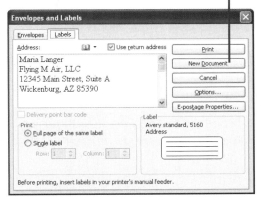

Word creates a new document that uses its table feature to create the labels.

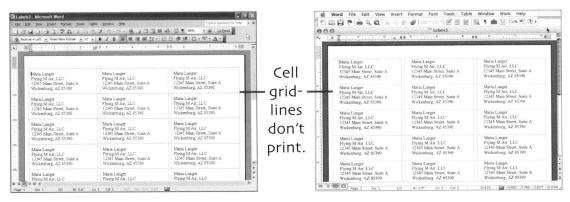

Cell grid-lines don't print.

Windows

Mac OS

finish your labels

When the labels are complete, you can save, print, and close the label document.

1 Save the labels. Use the Save command to display the Save As dialog and save the labels in a place where they'll be easy to find. Saving the label document makes it even quicker and easier to create labels. The next time you want to print labels, just open the document and print it.

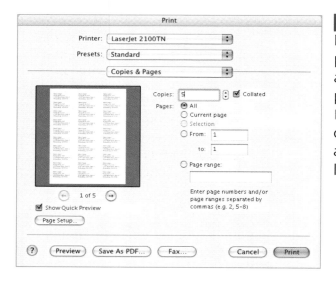

2 Print the labels. Insert the label stock into your printer's print tray or manual feeder and use the Print command to print them. Enter a value in the Number of copies (Windows) or Copies (Mac OS) box to print as many sheets of labels as you like.

3 Close the document file. If you're done working with the labels, close the document.

extra bits

open the labels dialog p. 124

- You must have at least one document open to use the Envelopes and Labels (Windows) or Labels (Mac OS) command. If no documents are open, click the New Blank Document button on the Standard toolbar to create one. You can then choose the Labels command.

select label product p. 125

- You can get the name of the label manufacturer and the product number from the package the labels come in.

enter text p. 128

- The Use return address (Windows) or Use my address (Mac OS) check box must be turned off to enter custom text in the Address box in the Labels tab of the Envelopes and Labels dialog (Windows) or Labels dialog (Mac OS).

create the document p. 129

- If you want to format the text of your labels, do so after the document has been created. Simply select the text you want to format and apply font and paragraph formatting. Consult Chapter 2 for more information about formatting text.

- If you don't want to create a label document—perhaps you just want to print labels quickly without saving them for future use—click the Print button in the Labels tab of the Envelopes and Labels dialog (Windows) or the Labels dialog (Mac OS). In Windows, the labels are sent right to the printer; in Mac OS, use the Print dialog that appears to send the labels to the printer.

index

index

D

Default button, 51
Del key (Mac OS), character deleting, 35
Delete key, 35
Delivery address box, 113
Delivery point bar code check box, Envelopes and Labels dialog, 116–117
delivery point bar codes, 117
dialogs, 11
  Break (Windows), 79
  check boxes, selection, 14
  Choose a Picture (Mac OS), 47, 52, 90
  Custom Page Options, 119
  Document, 41
  Document (Mac OS), Default button, 51
  Envelope (Mac OS), 113–114, 120
    Custom button, 119
  Envelope Options, 115
  Envelopes and Labels (Windows), 113–114, 120
    Labels tab, 84–85
  Font, 27, 46, 71, 88, 99
  Format Picture, 105
    Size options, 52
  Insert Picture (Windows), 47, 90
  Label Options, 85
  Labels (Mac OS), 84–85
  New Custom laser, 126
  Open, 17–18
  Options, 36, 56
  Page Setup (Windows), 41
    Default button, 51
  Paragraph, 29, 71, 73
  Picture (Windows), 52
  Preferences, 36, 57

  Print, 31
  Project Gallery, 55
  Properties, 107
  Save As, 38, 50, 61, 80
  Tabs, 73
  Templates, 54
dictionaries, adding to, 59
Document command (Format menu - Mac OS), 41, 77, 97
Document dialog (Mac OS), 41
  Default button, 51
  Layout button, 77
  Margins button, 97
Document option, Templates dialogs, 54
Document Template option, 50
documents, 15
  blank lines, 62
  closing, 34
  creating, 16
    business cards, 87
    letterhead templates, 40
    letters, 54–55, 62
    résumés, 66
    return address labels, 129
  flyer preparation, 96
  formatting
    characters, 26–27
    paragraphs, 28–29
  icons, 2
  letterhead templates
    preparing, 40
    setting margins, 41–42
  opening
    Finder, 35
    Mac OS, 18
    Windows, 17
    Windows Explorer, 35
  printing
    Mac OS, 31
    Windows, 30

  saving
    Mac OS, 33
    Windows, 32
  text
    copy and paste, 22
    cut and paste, 23
    drag and drop, 24
    editing, 19–20
    selecting, 21
  text area
    Mac OS, 6
    Windows, 5
  undo actions, 25
Documents folder (Mac OS)
  business cards, 92
  flyers, 109
  letter saving, 61
  résumé saving, 80
double-clicks (mouse), 3
drag
  mouse, 3
  text, 24
drop text, 24
drop-down lists, Windows dialogs, 11
duplicating business cards, 91

E

Edit list item, Mac OS, 37
Edit menu commands
  Copy, 22, 91
  Cut, 23
  Paste, 22–23, 91
  Redo, 37
  Undo, 25
  Undo Next Cell, 93
Edit tab, Windows, 37
editing text, 19–20
Education section, résumés, 70

index

index

index

index

Ready to Learn More?

If you enjoyed this project and are ready to learn more, pick up a *Visual QuickStart Guide*, the best-selling, most affordable, most trusted, quick-reference series for computing.

With more than 5.5 million copies in print, *Visual QuickStart Guides* are the industry's best-selling series of affordable, quick-reference guides. This series from Peachpit Press includes more than 200 titles covering the leading applications for digital photography and illustration, digital video and sound editing, Web design and development, business productivity, graphic design, operating systems, and more. Best of all, these books respect your time and intelligence. With tons of well-chosen illustrations and practical, labor-saving tips, they'll have you up to speed on new software fast.

> " When you need to quickly learn to use a new application or new version of an application, you can't do better than the **Visual QuickStart Guides** from Peachpit Press."
>
> Jay Nelson
> *Design Tools Monthly*

www.peachpit.com